Because

GRANPA

SAYS SO

that's why!

THE WIT & WISDOM OF GRANPA CRATCHET

LIVED & WRITTEN BY

SAM BOWMAN

Printed in the USA

Published by The Bowman Initiative, Sharpsville, Indiana

ISBN (print): 978-0-9983494-0-4

ISBN (Kindle): 978-0-9983494-1-1

Library of Congress Control Number (LCCN): 2016960217

Cover Design by Kristine Cotterman, Exodus Design, www.exodusdesign.com

Prepared for Publication by Palm Tree Productions, www.palmtreeproductions.com

To Contact the Author:
www.oldcoot.com

www.bowmanintiative.com

DEDICATION

This book is dedicated to the huge parade of funny people, and very serious people, who have come through my life and our house over the years, making Granpa the adventure of a lifetime. I can't name you all, but if you're out there and helped in some way I'd love to hear from you.

- First and most, to my mom who gave me my sense of humor.

- Next to the many, many performers, agents and shop workers who have contributed over the years. Just a few are Jason Fronczak, John Smith, Matt Taylor, Steve White, Chris Rafinski, Doug Long, John & Tula Pearson, George Moffett, Harrison Haney, Troy Burger, Jason Cook, Greg Bean, Jennifer Cook, Rick & Jolene Pickens, Rob Booth, Jimmy Rice, Dave Howard, Steve Carroll, Denny Bales, Denny Johnson, Mike Brody, Lanni Cates, Charlie Slavin, Bill Higgins, Wes and Vicki Oler, Ron Badour, Kevin Kolack, Travis Johnson, Jerry Hostetler and many, many more.

- To my wife Debbie, who married me without ever seeing me perform (Thank God), who stuck with me when she found out I played with dolls and continued to support me through all the disasters that now make up most of my Granpa stories.

- To all the five hundred plus, wonderful and faithful clients, who have consistently booked me and made life with Granpa possible, here's a few of the lifers:

  - Howard County Fair (My home fair, 28+ years),
  - The Sheboygan County Fair (26+ years),
  - The Whiteside County Fair (30+ years),
  - The Heart of Illinois Fair, who was the very first to book me,
  - The Nappanee Apple Festival (15+ years),
  - The Portage/Randolph Fair (20+),
  - The West Virginia Interstate Fair (20+),

3

- The Washboard Festival (15+),
- The Calvert County Fair (10+),
- The Black Walnut Festival (10+),
- The Fon du Lac Fair (15+),
- ... and many, many more who took a chance on me and trusted me with access to their most valuable asset, their kids. Life would have been a lot simpler if all you guys would have just left me alone! But then I wouldn't have created this book to put your name on.

● Last, but not least, to the grandparents who first saw Granpa forty years ago as little children and are now bringing their grandkids to see Granpa. Because of you I never age.

● Actually, all of you guys wrote this book and gave it to me for free. Well, here it is, back at ya. Could I have ten bucks?

● And now to Anthony, who again shows me what a sense of humor God has.

PRAISE FOR GRANPA SAYS SO

Sam is awesome. You should read his book. His life is one big joke, if you know what I mean, and I mean that in a totally good way. So, if you feel bad about your life, read about his, then you'll feel great about yours!

> —Rick Pickens: Puppeteer, Children's Pastor, Best Friend (So Sam claims)

When I first met Sam at Autoworld amusement park in Flint, Michigan he didn't know which end of the screwdriver to use. He thought a wrench was something you did to your back. I once handed him a cordless drill and he spent a half hour trying to figure out how to plug it in. It's a wonder to me he knew which end of the pen to use to write this book. But, most of the great stories in this book happened because Sam had no idea what he was doing. You'll really enjoy it, mostly because you didn't have to live it.

> —Ron Badour: Designer, Builder, Expert at Everything

Working with Sam I learned so much about how to work with kids. Mainly because he was such a kid. Working with him was like dealing with an eight year old. If something didn't work the way he wanted he would flop on the floor and kick and scream. I sure hope this book sells, or there might be a huge kicking/screaming earthquake in Indiana. So, please buy his book and save us all the clean up.

> —Travis Johnson: Puppeteer, Children's Pastor

Sam is great, especially when he's not walking into a wall or a plate glass window. His book will have you banging your head against the wall. Hey, Sam, Elvis gave his agent 50%, why don't you?

> —George Moffett: Super Agent, Variety Attractions

Sam is totally lost. I once had to turn Sam around and send him to the right state, but then his state of mind has always been questionable. How else could someone come up with all of this funny stuff unless something funny was going on in that brain of his. Maybe a bad sense of direction is part of having a good sense of humor and that part of Sam called Granpa Cratchet certainly has that. You need to have this book. It will get your funny bone going in the right direction and help Sam find Sam.

—Ken Woodward: Agent and friend, Variety Attractions

It was the summer of 1998. Granpa and I drove 17,000 miles back and forth across this great country of ours. The looks on people's faces when I would fly by them on the highway with Granpa buckled into the passenger seat or hollerin' at them out the window! I'll never forget the time some kid asked me if my name was Granpa "Cra-shay" and I said "What?!?!?! DO I LOOK FRENCH TO YOU?!?!?!" I was lucky enough to keep playing Granpa on and off for a few more years, 'cause hey, it got me out of New York City, the cleanest city in the world. I'm still not sure which is more fun, rolling through a cow pie or riding the NYC subway. Anyhoo, if you buy this book I suppose you can read it if you want, and after that, you can give it to your cat or use it to wipe your shoes, or anything else that needs wiping (if you know what I mean). So wipe that grin off your face and buy this book. It'll put a grin back on your face. It's worth the half dollar.

—Dr. Kevin Kolack: Actor, Puppeteer, Professor, and Student of Life

What can I say about my dad? He is creative. He's also sixty five years old and still doesn't know what to do with his life. So, he just goes full speed every direction he can think of. Is that creative comic genius, or confused insanity? In his case maybe it's both. But, in any case, the best thing I can say about my dad is, he's my dad. This book is great, but I'm his best creation. Always have been. Always will be. Love you, dad.

—Kimberly Lowe Bowman: Awesome Daughter, Entrepreneur,
Chip Off the Old Block, Best Creation Ever

Blah, blah, blah, blah, blah.

—Anthony Thompson: Three-year-old grandson
(his actual words when I asked him for an endorsement)

I married Sam without ever seeing one of his shows. My bad. Living with a guy that plays with dolls for a living (the living part is debatable), I could write a book about that! Oh, I did. It's called Debbie In Wonderland, or maybe One Flew Into the Kokoo's Nest. I've heard of split personalities, but a hundred and twenty three? It usually takes me all day just to figure out who I'm talking to. Sam's a character alright. Life with him is never dull (28 years and counting) and neither is this book. It will keep you interested just trying to figure out which of his inner characters is talking.

—Debbie Hale Bowman: Wife, Author, Mother to His Children
(mother to him most of the time)

I played Granpa for Sam for several years. What a trip! On one of my trips across country in one of Sam's Granpa Cratchet units the tongue fell off the trailer. I called Sam up and said, "Sam! The tongue fell off my trailer." Sam said, "So, what's the problem?" I repeated, "The tongue fell off my trailer." He said, "Stick it back on and get on down the road." So I did. You'll fall off your chair reading the outlandish stories in this book, and believe you me, they all actually happened. Great times. Great book. Love you, man.

—Bill Higgins: Puppeteer, Friend, Awesome Grandpa

Sam helped me get my big break in show business. For that I'd like to break his neck! Just kidding. Sam helped me find God and that has helped me survive life. Now you can help him by buying his book. What will you get out of it? The same thing I did. A lot of laughs and the inspiration to keep going.

—Brad Bodary: Fellow Performer, The Human Mannequin and Super Clown

When I first met Sam he was this little skinny guy with really big ideas. Now he's this really big guy, and has stayed true in delivering tons of laughter. Buy his book, put it on your night stand and read it when you've had a bad day. Then your day won't seem so bad! LOL, again!

—Steve White: Agent, Fellow Performer, Super Salesman

If I could go back in time and change my experience with Sam... Umm... Wait, Let me think... I wouldn't change a single thing! Sam has taught me so many things... How to perform in front of a large crowd, how to improvise... and most importantly - how to drive a camper truck with a long flatbed trailer! Truthfully Sam, thank you for teaching me how to be a better Christian.

—Mike Brody: Puppeteer, All Around Good Guy

This is the best joke book I have ever read. It's the only joke book I've ever read. But hey, when you don't know how to read, anything looks good. I did laugh a lot at the pictures.

—John Pareson: Puppeteer, Musician

I always told Sam he could do anything he set his mind to. He set it somewhere all right, now if he can just remember where he left it. I gave Sam his sense of humor. Heck, I gave Sam Sam. If you don't buy his book I'll talk to God about you. I see Him every day and I'm not here to tell you, He's real and I do have a great deal of influence, both here and there. Buy his book!

—Maggie Bowman: A posthumous post from Sam's mother.
Now deceased, but still influencing as much as ever

It still astounds me that Sam, as a single father in the middle of rural Indiana in the late 70s, started a puppet company that would remain his bread and butter for nearly 40 years. Sam's stories never cease to amaze me. Hearing him tell his stories feels almost as if I'm hearing 10 life times worth of adventures. I guess that's what happens when performing as Granpa Cratchet . I know you'll enjoy reading about it because I enjoyed hearing about it during my years as a puppeteer with Sam! And I can attest that these larger than life stories are indeed just evidence of how large a life one can live. Maybe someday they'll make a movie of your life, Sam. They should. You deserve it! Sell some books and send me some money for my pupaphobia counseling will you? But, we'll always have Sharpsville.

—Harrison Haney: Performer, Puppet Builder, Cartoonist

Sam is very, very funny as Granpa Cratchet. As a person he's as dull as saw blade that's been cutting through a pile of nails for the past month. The book is a lot funnier than you, Sam. If it hadn't been for all of us, you wouldn't have any story to tell. Ha. Read your own book. I wish you could have been as funny.

—Chris Rapinski: Puppeteer, Human Resources, Master Puppet Wrangler

Sam taught me his awesome life wisdom with things like, "Don't look at me in that tone of voice," or "Hey buddy, don't threaten me with a good time!" LOL And, I can't leave out the one I use most in my life, "Just do it." If you'd ask him how to wire up a space shuttle he'd say "Just do it." That's his answer for everything in life. I once saw him "just do it" round the clock, working in the puppet shop for three days straight without sleep. I read this book and it only took me three minutes to go right to sleep. But, he did it. He lived the life and then wrote a book about it. Hey, Sam. If you need to sell more books, the key is simple, "Just do it."

—Jason Cook: Shop Worker, Mentoree, General Pain In the You Know What, Farmer, World Class Business Man

Can you take me to lunch today?

—Joaquin Bowman: Sam's dad, now ninety two years old (actual quote from him when I told him I wrote a book)

Thanks for the memories, Sam. Actually, more like nightmares. Thanks for writing a book that will will remind me of everything I've been trying to forget. LOL. I loved traveling with Granpa and you'll love this book. Anyway, when the nightmares keep me awake your book will help put me right back to sleep.

—Jimmy Rice: Puppeteer, awesome dad

I wholeheartedly endorse this book. This book is awesome. You should buy a thousand copies and give them away. This is the best book I have ever read. Makes Tolstoy and Hemingway look like amateurs. I would pay a thousand dollars for one copy of this book and if I were you I'd give the author ten thousand dollars for just a few minutes of his comic genius.

—Granpa Cratchet: Comic Muse, Leading Man, Show Business Icon

Granpa's jokes land with the graceful tenderness and eloquence not seen since the Hindenburg crashed into the Titanic. No less than 72 of his jokes are powerful enough to guarantee you'll be both the life of the party and the cause of an apocalyptic size blow up with your in-laws - in other words - it's a WIN WIN!

—Cameron Bowman: Awesome Number One Son, Award Winning Videographer

9

Sam has a lot of faith. He has faith in people, faith in God, faith in himself. He built this whole Granpa Cratchet business on faith. Heck, he's still running it on faith. It took a lot of faith to publish this book. I'll bet he has faith that somebody will actually read this book. But what really impresses me is the faith it took for Debbie to marry Sam. Keep up the faith, Sam. Surely, somebody, somewhere will read this book sometime before the copyright runs out. Its not even out yet and I saw a copy in a flea market yesterday. Please be the one to read it so I won't have to.

—Jerry Hostetler: Builder, Repair Man, Master Encourager

FOREWORD

If you're one of the few who have never met him, Granpa Cratchet is a puppet. But, he's also a real person, the quintessential old person, full of in-your-face energy, trying to bridge the gap between the good old days and modern technology, good old fashioned family values and new fangled ideas. In short Granpa is all of us.

Granpa's award winning show has been appearing at fairs and festivals for nearly forty years. During that time he has appeared at over two thousand live events and presented over half a million shows. He has been seen live by millions. Besides that, he has appeared four times on the Today Show, Entertainment Tonight, Good Morning America and on every major network: ABC, NBC, CBS, PBS, ESPN, The PTL Network, the LeSea Broadcasting Network, the Success-N-Life Network with such names as Willard Scott, Dick VanPatten and Barbara Mandrel. He still appears around the world on several satellites on the Captain Hook Show, and the Kidz Television Network. It is estimated that he has made over one thousand appearances on local radio, television and newspapers and personally hugged over two hundred and fifty thousand kids.

During his highly successful show business career he has taught children his most valuable life rules rooted in the good old days. He has accumulated hundreds of insights and sayings while driving around in his Puppetmobiles™. His "children" are truly kids of all ages, anyone who is a kid at heart. He often says, "Everyone should be ten years old at least once a day," or whatever age the kid he's talking to at the moment happens to be. Kids love him for his love and hugs, teenagers love him for his in-your-face backtalk, parents love him because he teaches valuable lessons, grandpas and grandmas love him because he won't let anyone forget the good old days.

This book contains over 500 of his favorite sayings. It also includes tidbits about the old days and agriculture. It includes quizzes, silly ads from his general store, some really stupid jokes, and some insightful truths that will ring a bell deep in your heart. Read it to your kids, grandkids and great grandkids. It's a great way to talk about the old days and tell them some of your stories while you teach them a thing or two their mom's and dad's neglected to mention.

Of course, Granpa Cratchet is not a real person, but many are convinced he's real. When kids say, "You're not real," he always says back, "Hey, I'm a real puppet! If I'm not real why are you talking to me? Uh? Uh? Uh? Uh?"

Granpa's identity was born in Sam Bowman as he grew up on a farm with his grandpa, Sam Ramseyer, in Indiana, back in the 1950s. Granpa grew up in Sam's heart as he grew up on the farm in the heydays of the great rural America that once was. Granpa came of age as Sam performed him at fairs and festivals, in front of millions, for over four decades. Here, Granpa's wit and wisdom is captured for future generations Sam will never get to meet.

Along the way Sam and his Granpa Cratchet crews have had a lot of hilarious misadventures while traveling across the world. Some of those antics are captured here for your enjoyment. But, like Granpa always says, "You never visit Granpa's place without learning something." So come along now and have a laugh or two with the world's most famous, unknown character, Granpa Cratchet, and you might also learn something along the way about agriculture.

INTERESTING GRANPA HISTORY AND FACTS #1

It all started when Sam picked up a puppet at a local toy store to help teach children at church, not counting all the times Sam built stuff out of boxes as a kid back on the farm in Indiana

BECAUSE I SAID SO THAT'S WHY!

- ☑ If you're going to smile, go all the way and laugh! It's good for the soul.
- ☑ If you don't like who I am, stick around, I'll be somebody different in a little bit.
- ☑ I'm like anybody else, just more so.
- ☑ I'm so depressed my back porch has a mood swing.
- ☑ I'd be a perfectionist, but I'm just too darn picky.
- ☑ She stole my heart. And my teeth are missing, too.

Granpa and kids at Granpa's TV camp

- ☑ Laughing at is a whole lot better than fighting with.
- ☑ What came first, the chicken or the egg? The chicken. Because God wouldn't let a chick be born and grow up without a mother.
- ☑ How far can you walk into the woods? Halfway, after that you're walking out of the woods.
- ☑ If you're just thinking out loud, I'd rather you do it outside.
- ☑ At my age love is not blind enough. I have to turn off the lights.
- ☑ The best part doing nothing is having someone special to do it with, and I'm your man.
- ☑ Since I'm not sure who I am I get to have a lot of fun being someone else.
- ☑ I'm bad at keeping secrets and good at giving advice, if and when I can remember either.
- ☑ God bless America and smite some of the other countries.
- ☑ I love Grandma so much I've popped the question every day since we started dating in 1947: when's supper?

☑ I've decided to do nothing today, and I'm going to work hard at it.

☑ I've worked very hard at being a success. It takes a lot of work to do nothing and do it right.

Granpa Agriculture Quiz #1

(Answers to all quizzes are in the back of the book)

True or false? Each farmer in our country feeds over 150 people every year.

IT ALL HAPPENED BECAUSE:

Okay, so here's the deal. The question I get most often is "How did you get started doing Granpa?" That question has a lot of answers. Some events in my life were big and noticeable while some influences that set the whole thing in motion are barely noticeable, but still, every event plays a significant role in setting me up to invent and successfully play this character for nearly forty years. I want you to understand it's not just about the big Wow! event, but it's all about the mundane everyday choices that build your life and make it what it is. All your small choices add up. So be alert! Make all the insignificant choices good ones and guess, what? Success will find you and overtake you. So let's get started with the first one, and, I'll leave it up to your imagination to see how that particular influence caused it all to happen.

IT ALL HAPPENED BECAUSE:

Because I was born on a farm in Indiana.

GRANPA ON DRIVING

☺ If you don't like the way I drive, stay off the sidewalk.

☺ Hey the road's going straight, why not take a little nap?

☺ A policeman said my driving was so bad, he wrote me a season ticket.

- ☻ I got a ticket for double parking and I was square in that space. Of course, the guy in the car under me was kind of upset.
- ☻ Drive with Granpa and experience the big bang first hand.

GRANPA DRIVING RAP SONGS

- ☻ Granpa Cratchet is my name, if I don't crash it, it's a shame.
- ☻ When you drive near Granpa and live you're blest, move over in a hurry or be laid to rest.
- ☻ Why drive between the lines when you can cut through the yard and pay the fines.
- ☻ When you hear my horn you better run, or you'll end up with your teeth stuck in your bun.
- ☻ When you see the back of my truck, there's no time left, if you thought I'd missed you, you're out of luck.
- ☻ The fenders are rusty, the paint it flakes: The muffler is crusty, the chassis it shakes. But when it comes - to get up and go, it got up and went, please call me a tow.
- ☻ Whenever I see a bright yellow light, I push on the gas with all of my might.
- ☻ When I'm stopped by a man in blue, I say, "Here's donuts, now let me through."
- ☻ When it's time to stop, I know what it takes: I hit another car 'cause I got no brakes.

Granma's Show Trivia #1

(Answers are in the back of the book.)

What is the name of the chicken in Granpa's Chicken Pot Kaplowie show?

INTERESTING GRANPA HISTORY AND FACTS #2

Sam learned what kids really love when he took his puppets into Trewyn School in Peoria to entertain and teach the kids while a new library was installed.

IT ALL HAPPENED BECAUSE:

Because my Granpa rocked me in the old red rocking chair.

Like Granpa Always Says in Right in the Kisser:
Follow the golden rule, always treat others the way you
want to be treated.

The Misadventures of Granpa – Divine Inspiration or Stupidity?

There's a fine line between a divine idea and stupidity. The idea of Puppetmobiles™ made my success. It was an idea a guy named John Geddes and I came up with late one night while brainstorming about how to get our characters out of the stage and down with the kids. John suggested a tank, but we decided that was a little too militant. So, I sold the idea for a secret agent car, which I didn't have, had no idea how to build, and had no money to get, by sending a line art drawing to Fox Valley mall in suburban Chicago. I prayed they wouldn't ask for a photo. They didn't and I got the contract, to appear in just four weeks.

Ralph in his secret agent car

I went from bank to bank begging for money. I worked around the clock, built the thing in my neighbor's garage, and about overslept the day of the show because I was so stinking exhausted. That idea made me a million dollars several times over. Of course I spent it all trying to build the next best idea, but hey it's all about the journey, right?

16

Granma's Show Trivia #2

What is the name of Granpa's pet pig?

GRANPA ON LIVING IN A SMALL TOWN

◈ You know you live in a small town when you don't use your turn signal because everybody knows where you're going anyway.

◈ You know you live in a small town when you greet each dog by name and they all wag their tails at you.

◈ You know you live in a small town when you dial the wrong number and talk for 15 minutes anyway.

◈ You know you live in a small town when you can't walk more than a block without someone stopping and offering you a ride.

◈ You know you live in a small town when they roll up the sidewalks at sunset.

◈ You know you live in a small town when you go to church on Wednesday night just because there's nothing else to do anyway.

◈ You know you live in a small town when the name of the town is printed on both sides of the same sign.

◈ You know you live in a small town when the policeman turns on his lights and stops you just to find out how Aunt Thelma is doing.

◈ You know you live in a small town when the knock at the door is neighbors stopping in to get their dishes back.

◈ You know you live in a small town when the doctor visits you and doesn't charge you.

◈ You know you live in a small town when people stop in the town park for a community picnic without any advertising.

Granpa Agriculture Quiz #2

True or false? A milk cow belches 50 liters of gas every day.

INTERESTING GRANPA HISTORY AND FACTS #3

Sam's first professional, paying gig was at Northwoods Mall in Peoria, Illinois with a troop of fifteen kids doing music, about 1976.

Granma's Show Trivia #3

What is the name of Granpa's dog in the Right in the Kisser show?

IT ALL HAPPENED BECAUSE:

Because I had a lot of time with my grandpa when I was growing up.

The Misadventures of Granpa – Take the Plunge

On Ralph's secret agent car I had about forty flashing lights and some special effects on the sound system, but the big deal was a fire bell I

Sammy in front of childhood shop
... building stuff way back then

put right on the nose of the car. It was a real fire bell, a big red thing, and when I would ring it kids would jump right out of their Barney underwear. Well, I was driving through a mall this one time that had a jewelry show or something like that going on. I just remember a lot of booths and displays and the aisles were very tight and there were a lot of people. There was a big round fountain in the middle of the center of the mall with squirting water. It was very close going and I wanted people to watch out, so as I rounded a corner to

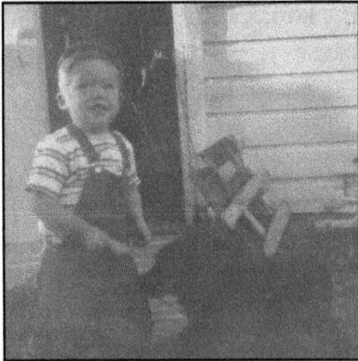

18

head down another wing I laid on the bell button. As I rounded the corner, what I couldn't see coming up in front of me was a couple of old ladies. I rounded the corner, laid on the bell and scared the wits out of the first old lady who stumbled backwards, bumped into the second old lady, which made her step backwards to keep her balance and she backed right up against the short brick wall of the fountain, lost her balance, and fell right in. Caplush! Fortunately the only thing wounded was pride and after some toweling off and a few free coupons from mall stores she went home happy. I'm so glad people have a sense of humor. It's saved my butt several times.

Granma's Show Trivia #4

What is Granma's pet dog's name, from the farmhouse show?

GRANPA'S FAVORITE CROSS JOKES

⇒ *What do you get if you cross a skunk with a boomerang?* A smell you can't get rid of.

⇒ *What do you get when you cross a church choir with a quarter pounder?* A hymnburger

⇒ *What do you get when you cross a snowman with a shark?* Frostbite.

⇒ *What do you get when you cross a hot pepper, a steam shovel and a Chihuahua?* A hot diggidy dog!

⇒ *What do you get when you cross poison ivy and a four leaf clover?* A rash of good luck!

⇒ *What do you get when you cross a cheetah & a hamburger?* Fast Food!

⇒ *What do you get when you cross a hula dancer with a boxer?* A Hawaiian Punch!

⇒ *What do you get when you cross a mini-cooper and an elephant?* A very little car with a very big trunk!

⇒ *What do you get when you cross Batman & Robin with a steamroller?* Flatman & Ribbon!

⇒ *What do you get when you cross a galaxy with a toad?* Star Warts!

⇒ *What do you get when you cross a strawberry with a road?* A traffic jam!

⇒ *What do you get when you cross a cow and a duck?* Milk & quackers!

⇒ *What do you get when you cross an octopus with a cow?* A farm animal that can milk itself!

⇒ *What do you get when you cross an elephant with a kangaroo?* Giant potholes all over Australia!

⇒ *What do you get when you cross a centipede and a parrot?* A walkie-talkie!

⇒ *What do you get when you cross a Karate expert with a pig?* Pork chops!

⇒ *What do you get if you cross a Cocker Spaniel with a Poodle and a rooster?* A cockapoodledoo!

Granpa Agriculture Quiz #3

True or false? There are more chickens in the world than people.

TRIPS DOWN MEMORY LANE
WITH GRANPA CRATCHET

A MUSTY PLACE IN THE BACK OF MY MIND

There was a special place that stood a little ways down the dusty, gravel road from where I lived as a child. It was a special place we called Granma's house. I say was, because it is physically long gone. Now it exists only in the recesses of my mind, in a special place reserved for warm childhood memories, ones just like the sights and sounds of Granma's house that stood just a little ways down the dusty, gravel road.

The memory of its smell still lingers though many years have gone by since I stood as a child just inside the back porch door. Every once in a great while I'll still wander into a room somewhere and a faint, musty smell of old wood, seasoned by years of cooking, or tobacco, or old newspapers will trigger a cascade of memories that will flow from that old place we called Granma's house, just a little ways down the dusty, gravel road.

As soon as you stepped inside the back porch door of Granma's house the musty smell of old newspapers stacked high and food cans that she had cleaned, smashed flat and stored in old gunny sacks, mixed in your nose with the smell of aged wood floors. The wood planks had soaked up some of the rich Indiana soil fallen from generations of old work shoes coming in from the rich Indiana fields. It was a potpourri of odors, special to that place that will never leave my mind, even though the house has long left the land.

There wasn't any running water at Granma's house. She wouldn't hear of it. Just inside the back door stood an old hand pump over a little tub that provided the water she needed to drink, cook and clean. A shiny tin cup hung on a nail above the pump. It wasn't a fancy, new fangled set up, but it was the best water you ever tasted: fresh and clean and cool on a hot day. Many times I stood by that pump mixing the taste of that fresh well water with the musty smells of the porch and that special formula forever etched itself into my mind

My great granma Stella Ramseyer's house down the road

and became part of the house we called Granma's, that stood just a little ways down the dusty, gravel road.

So when I happen to wander into an unknown place that has just a hint of that familiar potpourri, I travel back to where the sound of that squeaky pump and the gurgle of the fresh, cool water mixes with the smell of the old musty porch and, for just a moment, I leave where I am and I take another walk - to a musty place in the back of my mind, where I live again as a child, and for just a moment, visit a special place we called Granma's house, just a little ways down the dusty, gravel road.

INTERESTING GRANPA HISTORY AND FACTS #4

Granpa's voice is a combination of Jimmy Stewart's slur and Walter Brennan's gravel, actors most kids today have never heard of.

Granma's Show Trivia #5

What name does Granpa give Granma's pet dog?

IT ALL HAPPENED BECAUSE:

My mom made me laugh.

*The joy of the Lord is my strength at all times and in all situations
—Nehemiah 8:10 (SLB trans).*

The Misadventures of Granpa –
An Academy Award

I was playing the Indiana State Fair in the mid 1980s with Granpa in his barnyard, selling coloring books after the show for a dollar. I had a big line up after one show and the very last kid in the line was this little African American child, as cute as a button, about five years old or so. He stepped up on the bail of hay and just stared at me with big brown eyes. No dollar. He just looked at me and I looked at him and finally Granpa said, "Would you like a coloring book?"

He shook his head yes. So I held out my hand and said, "Okay, one dollar please."

He said, "I ain't got no dollar."

I said, "Go ask your mom for a dollar."

He said, "I did and she ain't got no dollar."

"Then go ask your dad for a dollar," I replied.

Then he said, "I ain't got no dad."

So I said, "Go ask your grandpa for a dollar."

He answered, "I ain't got no grandpa either."

The conversation stalled and we just looked at each other. Then big crocodile tears began to run down his cheeks and he said, "Will you be my grandpa?"

I thought, either this kid deserves an academy award or he's for real. I thought, either way, he wins.

So I said to him, "Sure. Why not? So now I'm your grandpa. So, go ahead and ask me."

He said, "Ask you what."

I said, "For a dollar. I'm your grandpa now so ask me for a dollar."

He said, "Could I have a dollar, grandpa?"

I said, "What for?"

He said, "So I can buy a coloring book."

I said, "Sure" and reached down into the money bucket and handed him a dollar and said, "There you are. Now tell me what you'd like."

He said, "A coloring book."

I said, "OK. Now hand me a dollar."

He handed me back the dollar and I handed him a coloring book and he broke out in this great big grin. With that he reached up and gave Granpa a big bear hug and said, "Thank you, Granpa."

That was thirty years ago and I've never forgotten it. Why? Because that's what it's all about; making a connection with a child, loving them and making them feel like they're somebody real special. I wonder if he still remembers our conversation as clearly as I do.

IT ALL HAPPENED BECAUSE:

My grandfather used to blow a steam whistle he had
hooked up to an air compressor in the shed.

**We estimate Granpa has
hugged over a quarter
of a million kids**

INTERESTING GRANPA HISTORY AND FACTS #5

Sam's first show featuring a lead character was Secret Agent Ralph, mild mannered reporter, who appeared at Northwoods Mall in Peoria, Illinois about 1978

GRANPA ON GOD

- ✝ God is like Coca-Cola - He's the real thing.
- ✝ God is like General Electric - He lights your path.
- ✝ God is like Bayer Aspirin - He works wonders.
- ✝ God is like Hallmark Cards - He cared enough to send the very best.
- ✝ God is like Tide - He gets out stains that others leave behind.
- ✝ God is like VO-5 Hair Spray - He holds through all kinds of weather.
- ✝ God is like Dial Soap - Aren't you glad you know Him? Don't you wish everyone did?
- ✝ God is like Sears - He has everything.
- ✝ God is like Alka Seltzer - Oh, what a relief He is!
- ✝ God is like Scotch Tape - You can't see Him, but you know He's there!
- ✝ God is like the American Express Card - Don't leave home without Him!
- ✝ It makes you wonder if the best products aren't ones that present some God like quality.

Granpa Agriculture Quiz #4

True or false?

Pigs do not prefer to sit in mud. Since they don't sweat they use the mud only as a coolant.

Granma's Show Trivia #6

Where does Squirt the skunk live?

The Misadventures of Granpa – Paint the Town Red

For a few years I did a lot of grand openings for Builder's Square. They had an eight foot wide aisle that ran in a square around the store they referred to as the track. It was great for driving Granpa's delivery truck around. For the grand openings they very zealously kept their track spit polished clean. It

Granpa at Builder's Square Grand Opening in Wisconsin

was the Builder's square square and they were proud of it. When I got there I'd clean, spit polish and double coat Granpa's truck with wax. Then I'd decorate the truck with items from the store, including covering the top of the truck.

I loved doing those displays. On this particular occasion I got the great idea of sitting cans of paint up on the top of the truck. At five minutes till opening I hopped in the truck and decided to take a spin around the track to get the old entertainment juices flowing. I rounded a corner, drove up to a couple of store workers and hit the brakes. Gallons of paint went sliding forward right across the waxed top of the truck, onto the top of the cab, off the front, falling down right in front of the windshield in front of me.

They hit the hood, rolled down the fenders, bounced off the running boards, and finally they landed on the floor. They bounced all over the truck and not a one opened until they hit the floor. Then every one of them opened. Associates from all over the store swarmed to the disaster and furiously sopped paint with rags. A few minutes later we all appeared at the front door to cut the ribbon and open a pristine store to the public without a speck of paint on any of us.

Granma's Show Trivia #7

What does Granpa's bathroom machine do?

INTERESTING GRANPA HISTORY AND FACTS #6

The first Puppetmobile™, Secret Agent Ralph's secret agent car, was created in my neighbor Tim's garage from an old golf cart and fiberglass. Later we found out you don't mix a flame throwing heater with fiberglass fumes. There's a funny story I'm glad we don't have.

IT ALL HAPPENED BECAUSE:

I was given roots.

Like Granpa Always Says in Right to the Moon Baby: Safety First! And second, and third.

GRANPA'S HOME REMEDIES

✦ Granpa's favorite home remedy: spank the kids

✦ Granpa's favorite home remedy: say I'm sorry

✦ Granpa's favorite home remedy: forgive and forget

✦ Granpa's favorite home remedy: commit forever

Granpa Agriculture Quiz #5

True or false? The average cow provides over 3,200 quarter pounders.

GRANPA'S FAVORITE PARADES

🔊 The Kansas City Parade for the Blind: Tends to wander. All the cheerleaders are covered in brail, lots of tripping, falling, head injury, Nobody ever sees it.

🔊 Wisconsin Cheese Cutter's Parade: Takes a long time because all entries are required to stop every fifty feet and cut the cheese. This parade stinks.

🔊 The Hicksville Old Fart Parade: Everybody has to wear long underwear with a flap in the back, carry their teeth in a jar and display their favorite itch cream on a tall pole.

- 🔊 The DesMoine Psychics Parade: it's really a sight to see, if you get what I mean. It's seldom seen. Nobody seems to know where the parade starts or stops, or where the route is.

- 🔊 The St. Louis Dentist and Orthodontist's parade: Instead of throwing candy they throw molars and bicuspids. It's like pulling teeth to get entries. The Cheerleaders twirl tooth picks and all floats must be covered with yellowed teeth. The band rarely plays in tune since it's hard to hit B flat with a numb lower lip. The parade's rarely been cancelled because of rain, but has been cancelled several times due to drool.

INTERESTING GRANPA HISTORY AND FACTS #7

Secret Agent Ralph appeared at many Jacobs Khan malls throughout the United States in his secret agent hide out, a complete building carried in the back of a cargo van and assembled in the mall.

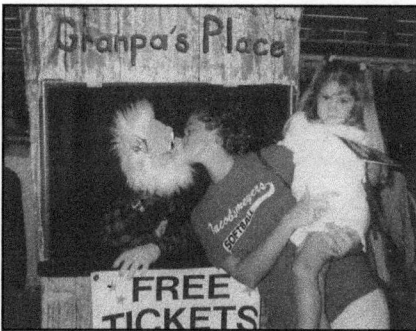

Granpa gave out a lot of hugs and a few kisses along the way too

STILL MORE SILLY PARADES GRANPA HAS APPEARED IN (NOT!)

- 🔊 Parade of American Assn. of Obstetricians, held down in Orlando: Parade is long. It lasts nine months. There's lots of screaming, and it features over 700 gurneys and a giant helium balloon that gives birth right at the corner of main street. What a mess.

- 🔊 The Atlanta Septic Tank Cleaners Parade: Featuring workers without whose valuable service we would all be a little grumpier. This parade often gets backed up and features honey wagons and manure spreaders. All floats are required to be covered in toilet paper. Cheerleaders do clog removal cheers. Instead of throwing candy they throw small rodents. This parade really sucks, in a good sort of way.

- Parade of North American Academy of Surgeons: Very funny parade, those guys are a bunch of cut ups. Instead of throwing candy they throw old body parts.

- National Assn of Proctologists Parade: Nobody ever sees it because it's always held where the sun doesn't shine.

IT ALL HAPPENED BECAUSE:

I gave my heart to Jesus when I was just a child.

Granma's Show Trivia #8

At Granpa's workshop he teaches: safety_____ ?

The Misadventures of Granpa – Open Mouth, Insert Foot

I've learned, but sometimes I still put my foot in my mouth. For example, I've learned you never ask a lady when her baby is due. Never. Never automatically assume a kid with long hair is a girl. Never. Always call the adult lady with the child mom, never grandma, no matter how old she looks. Never. Never, ever use the word ship in public. There's always some hard hearing old lady that will accuse you of foul language.

Still, sometimes Granpa has to push the comedy edge to tickle a funny bone and sometimes I step over the edge. Once I drove Granpa's mobile around the corner of the track in a Builder's Square store and there stood a tall beautiful brunette, dressed in high heels to the nines and her arms were loaded down with tubes of caulk. I blurted out, "You know I once caulked the cracks of Myra Barnfarthy. And she loved every minute of it!" Granpa did his usual belly laugh at his own joke and drove on. Later I got a call from Greg, the vice president of Builder's Square. He tried to ball me out for the comment, but then started to laugh. He gave me a get out comedy jail free card and I safely passed the Builder's Square Go on that one.

INTERESTING GRANPA HISTORY AND FACTS #8

As time went along more and more of the teens dropped out of the puppet troop until finally at one show no one came so Sam had to create a way to perform all his main characters all by himself. Since that time all the touring shows have been one man shows where one person does everything; set up, repairs, performance and road management.

STILL MORE OF GRANPA'S FAVORITE PARADES

- 🔊 The Plumber's Parade of New York City. Not mummers, plumbers. They dance around with toilet rings around their necks, there's lots of flushing and splashing. Everybody marches a few yards and then stops to take a leak.
- 🔊 The Pocupsie Rattlesnake Handlers and Snake Charmer's Parade: People are dying to see that one. There never is a second annual parade. They toss out snake bite kits and marchers regularly run into the crowd with knives to cut bite marks.

IT ALL HAPPENED BECAUSE:

My mom was a teacher

STILL MORE SILLY PARADES

- 🔊 The Scottsdale Headhunters and Cannibals Parade: You have to bring your own pot. Barbeque sauce is a great sponsor of this parade. The parade never ends because there's never anybody left.
- 🔊 The Sheboygan Annual Dancing Yak's and Twirling Clams Parade. They feature over 500 dancing yaks in the front of the parade, that way they don't have to smear the streets with Vaseline for the twirling clams.

Granma's Show Trivia #9

At Granpa's general store he teaches: the golden _____ ?

The Misadventures of Granpa – My Cup Overfloweth

I went on a talk show on the local Indianapolis Praise the Lord TV Network station. A man named Bob Silvers, who was religion editor for the Saturday evening post, and his wife, were the guest hosts of the show that day. They were both very handsome people, and were dressed superb for the appearance on a very elegant set. I got the great idea of creating a few laughs by having Granpa demonstrate his toilet paper machine. So I set Granpa and the machine between Bob and me and right as we were going on the air this guy comes over and sets three huge quart glasses of ice water right across the coffee table in front of each of us. The red light came on and Bob introduced Granpa. At the right moment I turned the machine on and, wanting to make a big comedy impression, kind of went out of control. The toilet paper dispenser, built out of this big leaf blower, roared into high gear and sent toilet paper all over the camera. I started wildly swinging the blower and completely wiped out the three 32 ounce glasses, sending freezing ice water flying. I soaked me, Granpa, Bob and his beautiful wife. Later Bob and I laughed about it all, but they never invited me back as a guest and never asked Bob to guest host again either. Just goes to show,

Sam on LeSea Broadcasting Network with Bob Silvers

if you're willing to embarrass yourself you can make a big impression on anyone.

Granpa Agriculture Quiz #6

True or false? A baseball is an agriculture product.

Granpa's General Store Traveling Puppet Theater

THIS WEEK'S GRANPA'S GENERAL STORE COUPON PROMOTION

This week Granpa's General Store is featuring Granpa's Old time Miracle Wonder All Purpose Ailment Elixir at 70% off, with the coupon from the Homegrown Gazette. It's a special blend of plant root, tree bark, extract of nut pulp, comprehensive mixed berry juices, herbs, spices, fruit skin squeezins and a top secret ingredient me and Granma discovered this past summer while we were cleaning out the chicken coop. Granpa's home remedy is good for warts, fever, indigestion, stunted growth and lack of hair. It also oils clock works, repairs broken dishes and elongates the life of vinyl, plastics and linoleum. Just smear some of Granpa's home remedy on your linoleum and you'll never have to wax again. Of course you'll have to find a barber that makes house calls. Just put a teaspoon of Granpa's home remedy in the rinse cycle of your wash and it'll heal up all the runs in your nylons.

INTERESTING GRANPA HISTORY AND FACTS #9

Sam partnered with Grace TV in Peoria in the early eighties where they created a series of puppet shows for local cable based on Secret Agent Ralph, mild mannered reporter. Sam also appeared as himself hosting a talk show for adults called Insight.

A Trip Down Memory Lane With Granpa Cratchet

THE OLD DINNER BELL

When I grew up we didn't have computers. We didn't have internet, or TVs. Heck we didn't even have a telephone. Today's kids can't imagine such primitive circumstances. What on earth did we do before the telephone? How did we get along! Back then facebook was called a letter. If you wanted to talk to someone you put on your shoes and walked to their house to sit down on the porch and talk for a while. Back then we didn't have a gas pump at every corner so we didn't go far, so you had to make friends with your neighbors, or you didn't have any. Or, another thing you could do was ring your bell. Not the one on your phone, the one on the post out back.

Way back then, you see, we had this big black bell on a post just outside the back door of our house. One day, as a kid of about eight, or something like that, I asked mom if I could ring the big black bell. So she replaced the old rotted rope with a new one and I tugged that bell for about five minutes straight and it left my ears ringing. In a little while we looked up and shuffling across the yard was an old lady in a long dark dress, with black high top shoes, wearing a big, fluffy old fashioned bonnet. I remember her name was Inny Davenport. She was our neighbor from across the road. Mom asked her, "Inny, what are you doing here?" She replied, "I heard you ringing the bell and I came as fast as I could to see what's the matter." Mom said, "Nothing is the matter. Why would you think anything is wrong?"

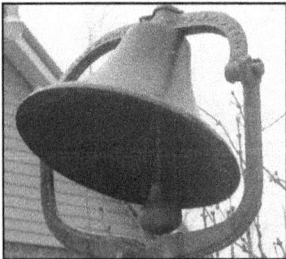

She then explained, "Well, when I was a little girl, if you rang your bell that meant there was an emergency and all the neighbors would run to the sound of the bell, whosever house that was." Even today we still occasionally honor that old time tradition by asking someone, "Does that ring a bell?"

Once in a while I'll hear a ring tone on someone's Iphone that kind of sounds like our old dinner bell back home on the farm. So not much has changed except now we carry the bell on our belts and when we answer the bell we can talk to anyone anywhere in the world. We have most certainly improved our technology, but I can't help wonder if we have really improved our world. Inny doesn't have to walk across the road anymore and I'm not sure that's a good thing.

Granma's Show Trivia #10

At Granpa's Farmer's Market he teaches: take the _____ out?

INTERESTING GRANPA HISTORY AND FACTS #10

Our first fair ever was with Secret Agent Ralph, at the Heart of Illinois Fair, in July of 1978. Granpa's very first appearance was at this same fair in 1981.

Sid and Susan bodyguard for Secret Agent Ralph

IT ALL HAPPENED BECAUSE:

I was raised in a house of faith. It taught me to keep going no matter what.

A FEW MORE REALLY BAD PARADES

- 🔊 The Annual Ft. Wayne Horse Apples and Cow Pie Parade: Held every October featuring the Shrine Poopper Scoopers. This parade is all down hill. The parade route is slicker than kitty poop on ice.

- 🔊 The Snapdragon Battle of the Cloggers Parade: Now that's something to see. There's usually lots of contusions and lacerations.

- 🔊 The Annual Poughkeepsie Porta Potty Parade: All floats must feature a black water falls display. During the parade they throw giant tootsie rolls into the crowds. You know how in Wisconsin they wear those blocks of cheese on their heads? Well I won't tell you what they wear on their heads in this parade.

- 🔊 The Annual Jacksonville Cat Skinners Parade: Cat lovers from all over the country come to see this one. All floats must feature ways to skin a cat. This parade route is short, but the floats all go through the parade route nine times. This parade showcases some awesome feline friends.

- 🔊 The Annual Peoria Cross Hatchers Clam Farm and Monkey Ranch Parade: All floats must depict a genetic experiment gone awry.

 *Granma's Show Trivia #11*
At Granpa's chicken coop he teaches: _____ together?

STILL MORE PARADE JOKES!!

- 🔊 The South Bend Horse Apples Parade: All cheerleader and twirlers must be costumed as a horse apple and all floats must be covered by some leaf or seed derived from the horse apple tree. This parade is all downhill, it can't be uphill. The street is just too slick. They have Carmel horse apples, horse apple pie and of course everybody's favorite, horse apple fritters.

- 🔊 The Semiannual Evansville Outhouse and Porta Potty Parade: all floats must be able to flush or double as a lady's bathroom.
- 🔊 Nobody wants to miss the 37th Annual Native American Indian Rain Dance Parade: Unfortunately nobody has ever seen it because it's been rained out for 37 years straight. They should put the rain dancers at the end of the parade. Its B.Y.O.B. - Bring your own brella.

Granpa Agriculture Quiz #7

True or false? One year's growth of fleece is about 8 pounds of wool.

The Misadventures of Granpa – Flying Super Hero

I was doing the Super Veg Man show at Parade of the Hills Festival in Nelsonville, Ohio. At one point in the show Granpa busts through the door as Super Veg Man and yells, "It's Super Veg Man of the universe, flying through the sky!"

Meanwhile some kids had gotten into the Puppetmobile I had parked behind the stage and pulled out the Granpa puppet. Swear to God, it's the absolute truth, right at the "Fly through the sky!" they launched Granpa right over the top of the stage. He came flying right down out of the sky in front of me and landed right in the middle of the little kids watching the show.

TaDa! Super Veg Man of the Universe!

All the kiddies started screaming and running off in all directions. It looked to them like Granpa had flown right out of the show and landed in a dead heap right on them! It took an hour to calm everyone down and get all the kids back with their right parents. More than a dozen little kiddies broke out in severe cases of harlequin phobia. Some were so traumatized they had to fly in a specialist in puppet trauma from New Jersey. For the life of me I cannot figure out to this day how they got that puppet to fly all the way over the trailer and why the festival didn't renew our contract.

IT ALL HAPPENED BECAUSE:

I helped my mom raise my brothers and sister.

INTERESTING GRANPA HISTORY AND FACTS #11

Granpa's first truck was called a huckster wagon, named after a truck that looked like a cross between a school bus and a gypsy wagon which Virgil Carter drove around the countryside selling groceries house to house from his store in Sharpsville, Indiana.

Granma's Show Trivia #12

At Granpa's farm house he teaches: follow the _____ ?

GRANPA ON THE WEATHER

- What goes up when the rain comes down? Umbrella, or Granma's rubber underwear.
- What did the tornado say to the sports car? Want to go for a spin?
- What happens when it rains cats & dogs? You might step in a poodle.
- Why did the blond go out with her purse open? There was a change in weather.
- What do you call it when it rains chickens? Fowl weather.
- It's raining so hard the ducks are heading for shelter.
- It's been raining so long the fish are hunting for a dry spot.
- Its been raining so long even Noah's getting worried.
- It's raining so much I saw a frog toweling off back there.
- It's been raining so hard I saw a worm using a hair dryer.
- It's been raining so long I flushed and my septic tank yelled stop that!
- Knock Knock. Who's there? Lettuce. Lettuce in, it's raining out here!
- What does a cloud wear under her raincoat? Thunderwear.

36

Granma's Show Trivia #13

What blows up at Granpa's workshop, in the safety first show?

Like Granpa Always Says In Chicken Pot Kaplowie: Work Together!

MORE REALLY WET JOKES

- ✗ It only rained three times this year: May, June and July
- ✗ It's been raining so long the fair is giving out sun checks.
- ✗ What did the dirt say when it started to rain? My name is mud
- ✗ It can rain cats and dogs all it wants. Just so it doesn't rain cows and horses
- ✗ It's been raining so long we're making Seattle look dry.
- ✗ I asked some kid if it ever stops raining. He said I don't know I'm only six.

The Misadventures of Granpa – On TV, Literally

Events often get publicity by having the local TV station do their weather live from the fair. This is often a one man operation where the weather man sets up his own equipment, usually a camera and a TV monitor so he can communicate with the station and see the weather graphics they put for him to talk about. On this occasion Granpa was given about thirty seconds to drive into the shot, tell a joke or two and to hype what was going on at the fair. So the weather man opened the weather segment, and introduced Granpa, who drove into the shot with his cool truck. We did our stick and I did the next

Granpa has appeared on local TV stations hundreds of times

logical thing, I drove forward to exit the shot. In
doing so I plowed right over all his equipment, camera, monitor and all.
That time I really was on TV, literally. That had to be funny for all the people
watching it broadcast live.

Granpa Agriculture Quiz #8

True or False? An automobile could not exist without farm products.

GRANPA ON POLITICS

- Best thing about politicians, never did meet one I couldn't dislike with a little effort.
- Only problem with political jokes: they get elected.
- Elections are like Christmas: they start too early, last too long, cost too much and then you still don't get what you want.
- I think my candidate is confused. I saw him on TV kissing hands and shaking babies.
- Congress is composed of two co-equal bodies: representatives who don't know the half of it, and senators who don't know the other half.
- God wants us to laugh. That's why he gave us politicians.
- Politicians are like diapers. They both need changing regularly and for the same reason.
- We'd all like to vote for the best man, but he's never a candidate.
- When I was a boy I was told that anybody could become President; I'm beginning to believe it
- Politicians are people who, when they see light at the end of the tunnel, go out and buy some more tunnel.
- How come we choose from just two people to run for president and 50 for Miss America?
- Politicians say they're beefing up our economy. Trouble is most don't know beef from pork.
- Why do politicians envy ventriloquists? Because they can lie without moving their lips.
- How can you tell when a politician is lying? His lips are moving.

- People now a days take their comedians seriously and the politicians as a joke.
- Some politicians do two terms - one in office and one in jail.
- I know how to balance the Budget. Declare Politicians as Game and sell Hunting Stamps.
- Political correctness? In my opinion nothing political is correct.
- Politics is like building a bridge, then digging the river.

IT ALL HAPPENED BECAUSE:

Grandpa Sam and Uncle Joe Ramseyer owned John
Deere 55 combines and I got to ride.

Granma's Show Trivia #14

At Granpa's barnyard he teaches: do your _____?

The Misadventures of Granpa – On Saying the Right Thing at the Right Time

Over the years I have had the privilege of meeting a few great men, and many more men that at least had a great title. Once the governor of Illinois stuck his head into the cab with Granpa and said, with great enthusiasm, as if I would be impressed, "Hi, Granpa. I'm Tommy Thompson, the governor of the great state of Illinois." Even though I have my hand in Granpa's mouth I never know what's going to come out of his mouth. Granpa shot back, "That's nice young man. Tell me this, are you a democrat, republican or a Christian?" To which he did not have an answer. After that all my state funding seemed to keep getting lost in red tape. I've made Granpa read "How to Win Friends and Influence People" several times, but it doesn't seem to do any good. Sorry Norman.

Granpa with Buddy Ebsen star of a TV sitcom The Beverly Hillbillies

INTERESTING GRANPA HISTORY AND FACTS #12

Sam met his first agent, Steve White, the very first year he performed Granpa Cratchet for The Heart of Illinois Fair in 1981. After that the business grew by leaps and bounds and as Sam says, his hobby became his headache.

GRANPA TAKES OUT THE GARBAGE

- Why doesn't a garbage collector like to go on blind dates? He doesn't want to get dumped.
- What is a garbage collectors favorite vehicle? A dump truck.
- Why don't garbage men have hobbies? Because they are already collectors.
- What is a garbage collectors favorite meal? Smashed potatoes, creamed corn, slima beans, mush melon, chunky soup and dump cake for desert.
- What is a garbage collectors favorite Christmas character? Sanitation Clause
- When a garbage collector loses a tooth who visits him at night? The goop fairy.

40

- Who is a sanitation engineers favorite winter character? Crusty the snowman.
- What happens when a garbage collector doesn't pay his bills? He gets a visit from the junk collector.
- What is a garbage collector favorite success saying? Stench by stench, life is a synch.
- Where does a garbage cop always go? To the scene of the trash. Or, to the scene of the grime.
- Why doesn't a garbage collector like to fly? They only allow two pieces of carry on garbage.
- What is a garbage collector favorite airline? TWA (Trash Workers Air)
- Why doesn't a garbage collector break the law? Because slime doesn't pay.
- Why do garbage collectors never die? Because they just waste away.
- Why don't garbage collectors like to pick up old clocks? Because it's a waste of time.

Granpa Agriculture Quiz #9

True or false? A milk cow gives over 100 glasses of milk every day.

IT ALL HAPPENED BECAUSE:

I went to a public school where they prayed before every day

The Misadventures of Granpa – Only In Hicksville

I once played a fair in a town named Hicksville. Absolute truth. Hicksville, Ohio. Look it up. No one had cell phones in the whole town because no cell phone service had a tower within twenty miles of the place. Nice people, though. The week I was there it rained all day long, every day, all week. I didn't do a single show the whole week. I felt bad for taking their money. When it came time to get out I hooked my truck up to the trailer and got stuck in the wet, soft ground. So they hooked a truck up to my truck and it got stuck. Then they hooked an old tractor up to their pick up truck. The motor on the tractor was so strong that when they popped the clutch the rear wheels of that tractor started spinning and completely covered the two trucks and my stage behind it with mud, and then promptly dug a hole so deep beneath each rear wheel the driver was sitting on the ground. So they brought in this big, giant caterpillar bulldozer and hooked a log chain to their tractor, which was still hooked to their truck, which was still hooked to my truck, which was still hooked to the stage trailer. The bulldozer was a ways up the line and sitting on a paved road so it pulled us all right out. One of the best parades I was ever in. Too bad it was raining so hard no one saw it. Honest to God truth. Really happened. It took me a week to dry out and get the mud out of my eyes.

INTERESTING GRANPA HISTORY AND FACTS #13

Granpa has appeared at over two thousand events. With each event averaging seven days, and an average of five shows per day, and up to seven units, Granpa has made over eight hundred thousand appearances before live audiences.

Granma's Show Trivia #15

In the chicken show what does Granma do to order chickens?

GRANPA ISM'S

- That ain't right.
- Shame on ya.
- Don't ya have no sense?
- Don't do that.
- Unbelieveable.
- Say purty please.
- Does your mama know ya do that?
- Have you seen Granma anywhere?
- Always remember, wherever yer at, there ya are!
  Something to live by.
- Hey, look at me. Do you think I have time for this?
- Talk to the hand.
- Granpa holds his hand out palm up and says, "Hey, give me five! Give me five. Give me five. No I mean five bucks. I need gas."
- Hubba, hubba.
- I can't hear you. I can't hear you. No, I mean I really can't hear you. Granma keeps borrowing the battery out of my hearing aid to run her electric train.
- This is my long time, good buddy, best friend, who I just met.
- It's time to get up and take a nap.
- Hey I exercise! I get up every day and walk around the block. I keep this block under my bed. I get up, take it out, walk around it, then push it back under the bed and crawl back in bed.
- It's grandma's fault.
- My retirement plan is sixteen grandkids with jobs.

Cast of Egg Yoke in the Underwear

43

INTERESTING GRANPA HISTORY AND FACTS #14

Granpa has remained the main character in all of the shows, with Cousin Clem, Granma and Fuzz Ball the dog rounding out the main cast, supported by as many as twenty characters.

THIS WEEK'S GRANPA'S GENERAL STORE COUPON PROMOTION

This week Granpa's General Store is featuring Granpa's Copper Clapper Cleaner, Coffee Creamer and Cockroach Killer at 70% off, with coupon from the Homegrown Gazette. It's is a special blend of plant root, tree bark, extract of nut pulp, comprehensive mixed berry juices, herbs, spices, fruit skin squeezens and a top secret ingredient me and Granma discovered this past summer while we were cleaning out the chicken coop. You can kill your cockroaches and cream your husband's coffee all at the same time. Of course, if he keels over while drinking coffee we know what that says about him!

Granma's Show Trivia #16

What blows up at the end of the farmer's market, take the garbage out show?

Granpa Agriculture Quiz #10

True or False? A baseball bat is a farm product.

The Misadventures of Granpa – Once In a Lifetime

Granpa is known as on grounds entertainment and is sold to events just like all the big, famous stars. One day I was just standing around at the Heart of Illinois Fair, in Peoria, Illinois, waiting to go on stage with Granpa and lo and behold there walking toward me was Bob Hope. I stuck out my hand and said, "Hello Mr. Hope. How are you?"

He shook my hand and said, "Fine thank you."

I don't know where it came from, but I blurted out, "Well, did you play well in Peoria?" (It was an old vaudeville axiom that if you play well in front of the conservative farmers in Peoria you could make it as an entertainer).

He replied, "Well, I think I did all right."

I said, "Bob, you might just have a future in show business."

He broke into a big smile and laughed out loud. I made Bob Hope laugh! A real high point in my life. Right up there with discovering you don't really need a root canal. All in all I'd rather get a big hug from a smiling five year old. That never fails to thrill my heart and I can do that any day.

Sam with the Kermit that played the banjo in the opening scene in the Muppets first movie

Granpa Agriculture Quiz #11

True or False? A hamburger is called a hamburger because it was invented in Hamburg, New York?

IT ALL HAPPENED BECAUSE:

I went to Huntington College, and majored in psych and made drama my minor because I thought I'd never do anything with it.

GRANPA'S REALLY SICK JOKES

- I'm so sick I went in for bypass surgery and my doctor said my heart was so bad he just bypassed the whole thing.
- I'm so sick I had them install a dimmer switch, so when I get all riled up you can just dim me down, and when I get depressed you can just dial me up.

45

- I'm so sick I have these blacking out spells, my left leg won't work, my right arm is numb, I'm legally blind in both eyes, but thank God I can still get a driver's license in Florida.
- I'm so sick I said to my doctor, "When I do this it hurts." He said quit doing that and charged me a hundred dollars.
- I'm so sick I put my hair on the bed post, my teeth in the jar, my glass eye in a cup, my wooden leg on the chair. You know you're sick when you can't remember where you put your spare parts.
- I'm so sick the first thing every morning I check the obituaries and if my name isn't there I get out of bed.

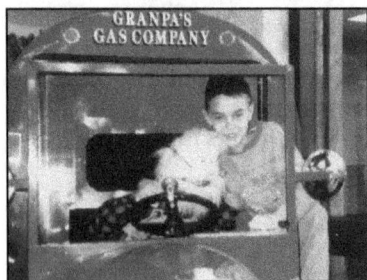

Speaking of being sick - Here's Granpa making a hospital visit while on tour in Texas for Exxon

- I'm so sick I went to a basketball game and when I sneezed my glass eye made a three pointer. Won the game for the home team.
- I'm so sick my doctor says I'm in very good shape for the terrible shape I'm in.
- I'm so sick my doctor said I have to walk around a block every morning. So, I keep this block under my bed, get up every morning, walk around it, put it back under my bed, and crawl back under the covers.
- I'm so sick my medicine takes medicine.
- I'm so sick I check with my mortician to see if I should keep my doctor's appointment.
- I'm so sick I can't go to the drug store without my trolley cart.
- I'm so sick I go to lobotomy support group on Tuesdays. I love those guys. They let me do all the talking.
- I'm so sick I keep a cardiac arrest team on speed dial.
- I'm so sick, I went to see my proctologist last week. When I saw the size of the bill I told him he could put it where the sun doesn't shine. I came out in worse shape than I went in.
- I'm so sick my proctologist had to use a shop vac to get my system going.

I happen to be drinking an extra large cup of coffee at the time and the whole thing disappeared in three seconds flat.

- I'm so sick I went to see my eye doctor, but I couldn't see him.

- I'm so sick I went to see my eyes, ears, nose and throat doctor and he couldn't tell which was which.

- I'm so sick, I keep breaking out in this rash, but hey it gives me something to do on weekends, you know what I mean (As Granpa is itching his neck).

- I'm so sick I have to take Viagra just to get up in the morning, and by up, I mean out of bed. At my age nothing will help the other problem.

- I'm so sick I keep the national center for disease control on speed dial.

- I'm so sick when my proctologist yelled "Hello" my you know what yelled "Hello" back at him, three times.

- I'm so sick I sneezed the other day and some of my brains came out.

- Oh, that's nothing. I'm so sick I sneezed the other day and my nose doctor popped out.

- I'm so sick my mortician gives me free haircuts.

- I'm so sick my mortician keeps a new suit my size hanging in his closet just to be prepared.

- I'm so sick my mortician watches my house with binoculars.

- I'm so sick I keep an ambulance on retainer.

- I'm so sick the doctor's receptionist thinks we're dating.

- I'm so sick I'm on a level payment plan with my mortician. Used him three times last year. He does give a great foot rub.

- I'm so sick I go down to the funeral home and lay in my casket just to break it in for the long haul.

- I'm so sick the mortician has me go around town and sneeze on people just so he can get more business.

- I'm so sick I sneezed so hard the other day my ears popped open, my back popped in, my hair popped off, my eye popped out and I had the best BM I've had in three months.

GRANPA SAYS, "HUMOR IS HEALTHY AND IT'S ALL ABOUT PERSPECTIVE. SO CROSS YOUR EYES, LOOK AT LIFE A NEW WAY AND START LAUGHING. YOU'LL LIVE LONGER."

A happy heart is as strong as medicine. Laugh and it'll keep you from wasting away. —Proverbs 17:22 (SLB trans)

Granma's Show Trivia #17

In the safety first show what food machine has Granpa invented?

LIKE GRANPA ALWAYS SAYS IN SUPER VEG MAN OF THE UNIVERSE: TAKE THE GARBAGE OUT ... AND KEEP IT OUT!

Granpa and his popcorn popper

The Misadventures of Granpa – Nose to Nose With Death – Or a John Deere

I was once contracted by producers to appear in an ESPN monster tractor/ truck pull TV special and live event in the Coliseum on the Indiana State fairgrounds. My job was to drive Granpa out into the area between pulls and do silly things to give the crowd something to watch while the next monster tractor got hitched up. At one point I decided to go ahead and pull out into the arena to be ready when the next monster finished its pull.

I tucked Granpa and his old truck mobile into the far corner and watched as the next monster, fire breathing machine dug in and began to thunder down the pulling track. However, the tractor began to veer off track and over toward me. On it came thundering like a locomotive, closer and closer to the very spot I was sitting. I thought it was going to run right over me.

I remember thinking I don't want to die in a Puppetmobile ran over by a monster tractor. It won't sound very impressive in an obituary, like dying from a rare disease or something. I instinctively did with the Granpa puppet what anyone would do, I put Granpa's hand up over his face and leaned back, like that would do any good warding off a twenty ton, smoke belching, fire breathing, earth eating monster going forty miles an hour.

That tractor roared right up to within a foot of my radiator and never slowed before it stopped dead cold, nose to nose, the giant machine with my tiny, little truck. Another foot and it would have bumped me. I parted my fingers and peered out. I could hear the crowd in the stadium laughing. The ESPN announcer ran up to Granpa and stuck a mic in his face and asked him if he was all right. Granpa said, "I think I'm O.K, but if you don't mind I have to go now and change my Sponge Bob underwear." The crowd roared and gave Granpa a round of applause as he drove out. The promoter loved it and the crowd thought it was all staged. What they didn't know was that I actually did leave and go change my underwear.

IT ALL HAPPENED BECAUSE:

Mom sent me walking down the road to great grandma Stella Ramseyer's house next door with a pie pan full of hot food.

Granma's Show Trivia #18

In Super Veg Man of the Universe how does Granpa become a super hero?

THE BURNING OF THE BARNS FESTIVAL

Granpa once used this script as a radio interview. Sam wrote this after his brother actually burned his barn down and the neighbors came over to watch. Really happened. You just can't get better fodder for Granpa jokes than real life.

Back home we have the "Burning Of The Barn" festival. It all started the year the cow kicked over the lantern in Fred Barnfarthey's barn. All the neighbors started gathering when they saw the smoke and somebody on the way home from the general store had hot dogs so they pulled them out to provide nourishment for the bucket brigade since the fire truck back in Sharpsville wouldn't start. Somebody ran home for mustard and pretty soon everybody was bringing in all kinds of food. Then somebody started pitching a ball to pass the time while the barn simmered, then somebody late that night got the idea of having a hymn-sing around the smoldering hay. Well three days later somebody said, "Hey this was fun, lets do it again next year." So ever since then come May we burn down somebody's barn, and eventually we called it the "Burning of the Barn Festival."

We are unique, we're not just yer average run of the mill festival. For instance, one of our big attractions is the pitch fork catching contest. Potential winners are judged on height, distance and length of laceration. Last year Little Earl Tellittall won the contest, he's the mayors son. Talk is political connections made the difference, but that's always true in pitchfork tossing.

Granpa did hundreds of radio interviews

We have bobbing for bowling balls. You have to have good suction to win this one. Last year it was won by Tillie Tellittall, the mayor's daughter. She has a big mouth and a way with bowling balls. For the five year olds and younger we have the tricycle demolition derby. Most events have a tractor pull, well we have a tractor pushing contest, our twist is the fact it's for ladies only. Won by Eunice Tellittall, the mayor's wife. She just gave it one of her looks and the tractor moved itself over the finish line. Course we had to repaint it, but it was worth it.

Most festivals have a watermelon seed spiting contest, well we developed that concept a little farther. We have the watermelon spit and catch contest. People come from miles around to see that one. There's nothin' like a 30 pound ball of watermelon guts nixed with a big wad of spit hitting a face full speed at thirty paces. Now that is entertainment. The perennial winner of that contest is Bula (Big Mouth) Tellittall, the mayor's mother.

The town isn't too big, only a hundred and forty three people, so everybody is on the committee. Ya gotch yer finance committee, ya gotch yer entertainment committee, ya gotch yer games committee and of course there's the "Last glowing embers committee." They are in charge of deciding who's barn gets burned to start the festival. Not a popular position, but one that needs filling. It you don't make a sizeable contribution to the festival coffers you can bet your barn will be on the potential donor list for next year. They also decide how the barn will be lit. You know the year they started the olympics with the flaming arrow? Where do you think they got that idea?

Granma's Show Trivia #19

What is the name of Granpa's home town?

IT ALL HAPPENED BECAUSE:

I was given three great children of my own to raise.

MORE BURNING OF THE BARNS

We do give people time to get their animals out of the barn. Speaking of hot pigs, one year Bill Barnfarthy mistakenly bought Viagra, which sounds a lot like Viagratone pig feed. He ordered and fed twelve hundred pounds of Viagra to his pigs. The next morning you wouldn't believe the sight. There were pigs stuck on fence posts, pigs stuck on trees, there were pigs on pigs and even pigs on sheep. Bill was scared to come outside. Now this has nothing to do with the festival, but it did spawn (sorry, no pun intended) the idea of having a hog roast. So we always have a big hog roast. We put a hog in a tux and set him up next to the speaker podium and then 40 or so people parade through for an hour or so and make fun of him. Last year the hog got to laughing so hard he shot slop right through his nose.

For the five to ten year olds we bring in a gator from Florida and have alligator wrestling. Ya, we're real education conscious. At the end of the fair we have a big gator wrestle off and the winner gets the gator, unless the gator goes undefeated. Last year the gator wrestle off was a tie, won by Bubba and Sissy Tellittall, the mayor's niece and nephew. Those are two mean kids I'm tell'n ya.

IT ALL HAPPENED BECAUSE:

I lost everything, twice, and somehow had the gumption to keep
going. (Garden Patch Dictionary defines gumption as: some unknown
drive, that refuses to give up, even when logic says give up, even
when momma says give up, even when the banker says give up,
even when the dog says give up, even when an angel comes in the
middle of the night and says, "Please, for God's sake, give up!")

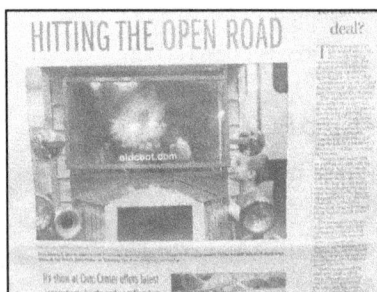

**Granpa has appeared in hundreds
of newspapers all across the
country—usually in the auto
accident reports section**

MORE BURNING OF THE BARNS

At the Burning of the Barn Festival we have the hot steaming cow pie toss.
One year we tried tying a bucket to contestant's chests and you had to toss
the chip into the bucket, move back three paces and toss it back to your
partner. It gave new meaning to the term bank shot. Now this is good, clean
family entertainment. Last year it was won by Thelma Tellittall, the mayor's
sister, primarily because you couldn't tell the difference between her and the
cow pie. No matter how much we wiped off her face she still looked pretty
much like a cow pie to us.

And we do cow tipping. A big sport with the young bucks. You sneak
up on the cow, ram her as hard as you can at full speed and try to tip her
over. Last year it didn't go so good. Ya, well the cow, unbeknowst to the cow
tipping committee had a bad case of constipation. Hadn't dropped a pie in
going on three weeks. Well, Fred Johnson Tellittall (the mayor's adopted son)
is a big kid, not only plays tackle on the Sharpsville football team, he plays
the whole front line, all by himself. He took a running start, hit the cow right

broad side and something jarred loose. Now we're not sure what that someth'n was, but it let loose. Totally loose. Yep, right there. Oh it was a sight. Have you heard of the phrase, "They didn't know what hit them?" We had to transport the whole audience down to the fire house and hose them off. From now on we're using a cork as a safety measure, a decision passed unanimously by the cow tipping committee soon after the incident.

The cast of Granma's Birthday Surprise at Granpa's farmhouse

Granma's Show Trivia #20

What blows up at the end of the farmhouse show teaching follow your instructions?

... AND THOSE BARNS KEEP ON BURNING ...

At the Burning of the Barn Festival we also have cow chip bingo. We spray paint squares on the ground and number them, then people bet where the chip will land when the cow goes to the bathroom. Winner takes all. Well, unbeknowst to the cow bingo committee, the cow had a bad case of the runs. Oh ya. It went all over the place. Everybody won. Nearly broke us.

And, we have a queen contest, for the honor of becoming Miss Fire Hydrant. We look for a short stocky girl and a lot of drooling goes a long way with the judges. We also look for intelligence, every year they have to write an essay on; "Your favorite fire hose and you." It's very educational for the girls. It's been won three years running by Ima Tellittall, the mayor's sister.

Last year our big music group was the Electric Amish. They played their new hit, "I got the blackout blues." If you play it backwards you can hear a voice saying, "Get a telephone." It's real cutting edge out on the farm. It didn't sell big though. Their record company was Outhouse Records, where the music is as good as it smells and every record has two holes.

We have some great carnival rides we bring in. There's the bun buster, the barf-o-wheel, and my favorite the puke-o-tilt. It's the American way to have fun and pay good money to do it too.

Every year we build the festival a little bigger and little better. Next year we hope to finish the needle in the haystack contest we started way back in 1972. Check our press release prepared by Gloria Gladgossip our Homegrown Gazette editor and first cousin, by marriage, to Mayor Tellittall.

The Misadventures of Granpa – The Today Show Goof

Granpa was on the Today Show with Willard Scott live from the San Antonio Livestock Show in Texas. Willard asked, "What kind of truck is this Granpa?"

To which Granpa replied, "A GMC."

Willard asked, "What's that mean?"

Granpa with Willard Scott

And Granpa says, "That means it takes a lot of God, money and credit to keep her on the road."

They both laughed it up and went right on with the weather. Later my agent Steve White called in a tizzy and wanted to know whose name my house was in. GMC was threatening a law suit over the joke. Within an hour of the interview we were on a conference call with a vice president of GMC from New York City and he read us the riot act for telling that joke on national TV.

He yelled, "Do you know how many people are making a decision that day whether or not to buy a GMC?!! You could have cost us hundreds of decisions and as much as five million dollars!"

I said, "I didn't realize. Do you really think the impact was that big?"

He said, "Oh yes, definitely, the impact could be huge!"

So I said, "Wow! If Granpa can make that big of an impact then we need to talk national sponsorship!"

I spent the next five minutes laying out all Granpa could do for them for a five million dollar national ad campaign. We never heard from them again.

Granpa Agriculture Quiz #12

True or false? One pound of wool can make ten miles of yarn.

Granma's Show Trivia #21

In the barnyard show what is the name of the chicken?

INTERESTING GRANPA HISTORY AND FACTS #15

The business expanded to two units in the mid 1980s and then to seven units in 1990, including seven trucks, seven campers, nine Puppetmobiles™, with sets, props and a supporting cast of more than a hundred characters.

GRANPA'S FAVORITE KNOCK KNOCK JOKES

Knock Knock – Who's there? Tom Sawyer. Tom Sawyer who?

Tom saw your underwear!

Knock Knock – Who's there? Anna. Anna who?

Annabody you want it to be.

Knock Knock – Who's there? Ashley. Ashley who?

Ashley I have no idea.

Knock Knock – Who's there? Harry. Harry who?

Harry Up and answer the door.

Knock Knock – Who's there? Ben. Ben who?

Been knocking so long my hand hurts.

Knock Knock – Who's there? Dwayne. Dwayne who?

Dwayne the bathtub I'm drowning.

Knock Knock – Who's there? Howard. Howard who?

Howard was it to find me?

Knock Knock – Who's there? Who. Who who?

Hey, did you hear that owl?

Granpa and Grace

Knock Knock – Who's there? Boo. Boo who?

Oh quit whining you big sissy!

Knock Knock – Who's there? Choo. Choo who?

God bless you. You have a cold?

Knock Knock – Who's there? Me. Me who?

If you don't know I sure as heck don't.

Knock Knock – Who's there?   Ha, ha, ha. Who ha, ha, ha?

Did I say something funny?

Knock Knock – Who's there? What, when & where? What, when & where who?

I didn't know you were a detective.

Knock Knock – Who's there? Knew. Who knew who?

I sure didn't so I was hoping you did.

IT ALL HAPPENED BECAUSE:

I was taught that the Bible was the book to live by

Granma's Show Trivia #22
In the barnyard show what is the name of the cat?

Granpa Agriculture Quiz #13
True or False? A cow has four stomachs.

THIS WEEK'S GRANPA'S GENERAL STORE COUPON PROMOTION

This week the Granpa's General Store is featuring Granpa's Fat Hog Feeds at 70% off, with coupon from the Homegrown Gazette. It's a special blend of plant root, tree bark, extract of nut pulp, comprehensive mixed berry juices, herbs, spices, fruit skin squeezens and a top secret ingredient me and Granma discovered this past summer while we were cleaning out the chicken coop. And, it'll also fatten up grandchildren just as well. But, don't blame me when they start acting like pigs at the dinner table.

The Misadventures of Granpa –
On Blowing Things Up

I built this cool metal box and put a lot of dials and buttons on it and called it Special Agent Ralph's computer. I think the skit was about following the instructions. Anyway, it was wired as a flash pot with gun powder and it would blow up and create a flame and a big puff of smoke, which was part of the skit. This particular time, as I was setting up, I thought I would test it out and make sure everything was in working order. So I set up the fuse, turned the igniter button on and saw the tiny wire burn out like it should.

PROVERBS 1:26 – I, THE LORD, WILL LAUGH IN THE MIDST OF ALL YOUR HARD TIMES; I LAUGH AT EVERYTHING YOU FEAR. (SLB TRANS)

Very sure of myself I rewired it and loaded it up with extra gun powder thinking I'm really going to impress these people. What I didn't know was that when I tested it I blew a breaker at the back of the auditorium and I also left the igniter switch in the on position. During the show I arrived at the punch line, pushed the button and nothing happened. So, I improvised and had Special Agent Ralph pick it up and lower it down to back stage so I could look in at it and see if the fuse wire had gotten loose. Meanwhile some guy in the sound booth at the back thought to check the breaker, saw it was tripped. I stuck my face right into the flash box and looked at the igniter wire at the very moment he reset the breaker. It worked perfectly. The flash pot went off right in my face. A huge flame shot up and a nice big cloud of smoke rolled up and around my head. I realized the excellent silliness of the Looney Toons moment, but was at the same time disappointed the audience didn't get to see it happen. I hate missing a chance for a good laugh. It only took about a month for my eyebrows to grow back. I got comments about my sun burn for several days after that. After trying about ten other really nasty tasting ideas I finally got the gun powder, sulfur residue taste out of my mouth by eating a giant raw onion and washing it down with a bottle of Listerine.

INTERESTING GRANPA HISTORY AND FACTS #16

The largest single year of performances was in 1994. With seven units in full swing, Granpa appeared at 107 events, averaging seven days per event and six shows per day, totaling 107 weeks, over seven hundred performance days and over four thousand shows all across the United States. Most of these were in a twelve week period.

IT ALL HAPPENED BECAUSE:

So many, many people helped.
Each of whom I consider to be a gift from God.

YOU THINK YOU'RE SO SMART, ANSWER ME THIS

- ✬ What is full of holes, but can still hold water?   A sponge.
- ✬ Imagine you are in a sinking rowboat surrounded by sharks. How would you survive? Quit imagining.
- ✬ What is light as a feather, but no one can hold for more than a few minutes? Your breath.

- What can run, but never walks, has a mouth but never talks, has a head but never weeps, and has a bed but never sleeps?   A river.
- What in an automobile engine serves no purpose, but without it the engine does not work? The noise.
- A man left home running. He ran a ways and then turned left, ran the same distance and turned left again, ran the same distance and turned left again. When he got home there were two masked men. Who were they? The catcher and the umpire.
- Why is it against the law for a man living in North Carolina to be buried in South Carolina? Because he's still living.
- Which is heavier: a pound of gold or a pound of feathers? Answer: feathers, because gold is weighed in 12 oz troy while feathers are weighed in 16 ounce Avoirdupois pounds.

Granpa Agriculture Quiz #14

True or false? Pig heart valves have been used to replace damaged human heart valves.

Adults love Granpa as much as kids. This is Dale. He was the original talent scout for The Tonight Show with Steve Allen and with Johnny Carson

- A man and his son were in an automobile accident. The man died on the way to the hospital, but the boy was rushed into surgery. The emergency room surgeon said "I can't operate, that's my son!" How is this possible? The surgeon was his mother.
- What came first, the chicken or the egg? The chicken because God wouldn't let a chick be born without a mother to raise it.
- How far can you walk into the woods? Halfway, after that you're walking out of the woods.
- What goes clop, clop, bang, bang, clop, clop, bang, bang clop, clop, bang, bang, clop, clop, bang, bang? A drive by Amish shooting.

INTERESTING GRANPA HISTORY AND FACTS #17

Granpa has appeared live in 45 of the United States and in Canada, Mexico, Panama and South Korea.

The Misadventures of Granpa – The Secret to Success: Out of Control

Our first mobile was a secret agent car we used with our mall show. It was built on an old golf cart that you drove with a stick. I got in by lifting up the lid, crawling in like a space capsule, then closing the lid back over myself. I would finish the stage show with a big bang and then invite the kids to meet Special Agent Ralph in his secret agent car. I'd run out the back of the stage, put on the puppet, close myself in, drive around front and begin shaking hands with kids in an orderly manner. It worked great, most of the time.

Once I had a huge crowd of school kids at a mall. I finished the show, ran out the back, closed myself in, reached under to grab the stick so I could drive, but the stick was gone! Somehow the stick had gotten stuck up under the body frame to the far left. The kids got impatient before I could fix the problem and began to throng out of control around the stage. They swarmed all over the car and the puppet like ants over a dead pig, patting and grabbing at him. I felt the puppet lift off my arm and float away into the sea of a hundred eight year old, screaming piranha. I never saw that Special Agent Ralph puppet again. I'm sure he's still on mission somewhere, all 300 pieces of him. Out of control still makes me break out in a cold sweat. But I've learned that when all else fails and I've got to have a breakthrough, a little out of control might be just the thing.

IT ALL HAPPENED BECAUSE:
I was taught to build things.

Granpa Agriculture Quiz #15

True or false? There are 150 yards (450 feet) of wool yarn in a baseball.

Like Granpa Always Says in his movie,
Granma's Birthday Surprise:

Follow the Instructions!

GRANPA'S FAVORITE BLOND JOKES

☺ Why don't blonds eat pickles? Because they keep getting their heads stuck in the jar.

☺ How do you make a blond laugh on Monday? Tell him a joke on Friday.

☺ Why don't blonds make Kool Aid? They can't figure out how to get eight glasses of water into one of those little packets.

☺ How do you get a blonds' eyes to sparkle? Shine a light in her ear.

☺ Why did the blond climb the chain link fence? To see what was on the other side.

☺ Why did the blond stare at the frozen orange juice for two hours? It said concentrate.

☺ Why did the blond put his finger over the nail while hammering? So the noise would stop giving him a headache.

☺ How does a blond know if he's on his way home or on his way to work? He opens his lunch box to see if there is anything in it.

☺ Why did the blond stop drinking milk? The cow sat down.

☺ What does a blond do when someone says its chilly outside? She grabs a bowl.

☺ Why don't blonds get mad cow disease? You can't get it twice.

☺ What goes stop, start, stop, start, stop, start? A blond driving through a blinking light.

☺ Why don't blonds make ice cubes? They don't know the recipe.

☺ What do you call 3 blonds that walk into a building? An opportunity for an ambulance to make money.

INTERESTING GRANPA HISTORY AND FACTS #18

Granpa has appeared on four satellites around the globe as part of The Captain Hook Show and the Kidz Television Network.

IT ALL HAPPENED BECAUSE:

John Geddes gave me his best ideas.

TRIPS DOWN MEMORY LANE WITH GRANPA CRATCHET

COFFEE IN THE SAUCER

Some of my fondest memories come from around the old oak kitchen table at which my family shared decades of meals or played games on snowy winter days. It was brought from Innie Davenport's house across the road when she had passed away and it was at that table that many memories were poured into my heart over the years. It was here that I sat with my mom and dad for seven years before my brothers and sister came along and sat in the same high chair that I had used. Later when I was a full grown man I sat again at this same table with my own children where the bountiful banquet of old fashioned cooking filled my empty stomach and the banter of our loving family filled the empty place in my heart when I had lost my wife and youngest son.

When I was little, Grandpa would come in from working on the farm for a noon meal of fried potatoes, sausage, corn on the cob and green beans. Of course there was always a strawberry or pumpkin pie and no meal was complete without a cup of hot steaming coffee fresh roasted in an old fashioned percolator on the top of the coal-burning stove. During the heavy work seasons, when it was time for planting in the spring or harvest in fall, the meals had to be quick, but still there was always the cup of hot steaming coffee. Mom would pour and then Granpa would add enough sugar to support a whole ant hill or send a perfectly calm child to removing the wallpaper on at least three rooms. He would stir for a bit and then tap the spoon on the edge of the rim and lift the hot steaming cup, not to his lips, but to pour onto the saucer. He would blow on the coffee as he poured and then pour from the saucer back to the cup and never spill a drop. Back and forth he would pour and blow until the steam began to fade. Then he would lift the saucer to his lips and sip the coffee that hand been cooled just right by his perfected cooling method, accumulated from many years of coffee calculating and temperature testing. He knew just when he could sip, his lips protected from burn by his cup to saucer pouring technique.

Time has gone by, but Mom still keeps some cookies or a pie sitting on the table's red and white checked oilcloth cover, ready to satisfy the need for a quick pick me up morsel for those who pass by. I can still see Grandpa sitting at the table on a matching old oak chair, in his overalls and white hair, pouring his coffee back and forth from here to there and back to here again and I realize how much that table brought to our lives. It's where we poured our hurts and our dreams back and forth into each other until they came of age, just right to be tasted and perfect for partaking.

Granpa has long since passed on and we have long grown up and hurried out the door, just like he did on those busy harvest days. But I'll always remember his pouring and sipping and be grateful for the love we poured into each other while eating together at that old kitchen table, that was bought from the house across the road when I was just a little boy.

Granma's Show Trivia #23

In the barnyard show what is the name of the rat?

A FEW OF GRANPA'S FAVORITE BUMPER STICKERS

- 🚗 What State Am I In - Besides the State of Confusion?
- 🚗 I Don't Use My Turn Signals Because I Don't Know Where I'm Going Anyway.
- 🚗 Don't Tailgate or I'll Flush.
- 🚗 If You Don't Like the Way I Drive Stay Off the Sidewalk.
- 🚗 Why Drive Inside the Lines When I Can Cut Through the Bushes and Pay the Fines?

Granpa Agriculture Quiz #16

True or False? 3 out of every 5 people earn at least part of their income from agriculture.

THE MISADVENTURES OF GRANPA - GRANPA CRASH-IT

This one time I was filming a commercial with Granpa out on the lot of Shield's Auto Center, a car dealership in Rantoul, Illinois. This car came

Sam shoots a TV commercial at Shield's Auto Center

driving by so I held up Granpa and had him wave at the driver. She smiled and slowed down to get a better look at what was going on. Evidently the guy in the car behind her was also looking over at the TV crew and puppet, but he didn't slow down and rear ended the girl. He hops out, runs up to her car and starts yelling at the girl and she starts crying. I whisked the puppet into his storage trunk and disappeared in a hurry thinking when she blamed me this guy was going to come over and pound Granpa or worse, slug me. I wonder how they explained it all on the police report without mentioning the waving "dummy?" I'm not sure which one of us was the real dummy.

IT ALL HAPPENED BECAUSE:

When I grew up I didn't have any electronics to distract me
from developing creativity.

Granpa Agriculture Quiz #17

True or false? Cows drink a bathtub full of water every day.

GRANPA ON HIS GIRL FRIENDS

- ♥ She rolled her eyes at me . . . and I rolled them right back.
- ♥ She had the most beautiful long hair, all the way down her back. She was bald on top, but had this thick black hair growing out of her back, all the way down.
- ♥ She had the most beautiful white tooth. That's it.
- ♥ She had this most gorgeous long leg, the other one was kind of short, but the long one was great!
- ♥ Some women have an hour glass figure, she had the whole clock.
- ♥ Back home in Sharpsville they called her a bag date. She was so ugly she had to wear a bag over her head so the guys would go out with her.
- ♥ Back home in Sharpsville they had double bag dates. That's where the girl is so ugly they have to put one bag on her head and one on his just in case her's blows off.
- ♥ She had the perfect nose right under her chin.
- ♥ Some people have quadruple heart bypass, she had quadruple chin bypass. They thought getting them all in a row would help.
- ♥ She went to have her ears pierced, but they couldn't find one for her chin.
- ♥ She did have her belly button pierced, to her ear, it was a nice fit.

Cousin Elem's Show Trivia #24

In the farmhouse show what are they celebrating?

The Misadventures of Granpa – The Great Disappointment That Validates My Craft

Over my forty years in show business I have had thousands of kids and adults beg me for a glance back stage and I always hesitate to do so, not because I'll give away my secrets, but because I know when they see the emptiness it will burst their bubble. It's always interesting to watch their smiles fade when they see there's nothing there. They expect to see a stairs or Granpa's fully decorated house and instead all they see is an empty space with puppets hanging around. It never ceases to amaze me how animating Granpa can create a whole imaginary world, where what the people see in their minds is more powerful than reality. The secret to my success is not so much what I actually do in front of people, but what I create in their imagination. If I can capture their imagination just once, I'll have their heart forever. If after the smile fades, it starts to come back again when they get it, I know I've got them.

IT ALL HAPPENED BECAUSE:

Roger Birdsall assigned me to work with the kids in children's church.

Granpa Agriculture Quiz #18

True or false? Horses have the largest eyes of any land mammal.

GRANPA STINKING RV PERMITS

📑 Have a party any stinking time, any stinking place permit: allows the holder of the permit to carry any and all party items and stop his or her recreational vehicle any stinking place he or she wants and party down baby.

66

📄 Relax any stinking time, any stinking place you want permit: allows the holder of the permit to remove his shoes or any other garment of his or her choosing, under or outer, make a cup of coffee, watch TV and do anything else they stinking well want whenever and wherever they want. In nothing at all if they want.

📄 Don't need no stinking public bathroom permit: allows the holder of the permit to stop his or her recreational vehicle any stinking place he or she wants and do #1 or #2 any stinking time he or she stinking wants.

📄 Live at any stinking Walmart you want permit: allows the holder of the permit to park his or her recreational vehicle any stinking place he or she wants for the duration of whatever.

**The Bellamy Brothers
get Granpa's
autograph**

TRIPS DOWN MEMORY LANE
WITH GRANPA CRATCHET

THE ART OF TENT BUILDING

When I was a kid we used to love to make tents. We made tents out of all kinds of things. I remember one time we got a new dryer that came in a big box. When the dryer came out I went in. I used to love to pack things into that box like pillows, magazines and whatever else I could find.

On the farm at that time we had these little wooden houses we used to keep our pigs in. They were only about six feet tall in front, with a flat slanted roof toward the back. They had a little vertical door in the front corner that made a perfect walk in door for a small fry. It also had a long horizontal door across the front that hinged down we used as a window, normally used to put fresh straw or food through to a sow and her little pigs. Grandpa Ramseyer pulled one up into the yard and we hosed it out, painted it white inside and out and it became our permanent play house. We had little chairs and a table and we used dishes my sister Susan had received as Christmas toys. We carted in old silverware, empty food cans, old cereal boxes and put up curtains out of old scraps of cloth. Anything we could get our hands on we used to set up house and decorate. At meal time we'd carry our sandwiches in a bag and sweet tea in jars out to the playhouse and pretend we were grown ups.

IT ALL HAPPENED BECAUSE:

Steve White saw the value of my idea and performance.

PROVERBS 3:5 – TRUST IN THE LORD WITH ALL YOUR HEART; AND TRUST NOT IN YOUR OWN UNDERSTANDING, IT'LL DISAPPOINT YOU EVERY TIME. (SLB TRANS)

We didn't have cell phones, I-pods, CD's or videos so we wiled away the summer hours working together making tents and playing house. Our playhouses were filled with lots of old junk, but perhaps they are so memorable because they were also filled with each other and lots of imagination. We learned a lot about building homes and lives as we built those tents in the dog days of summer back when we were kids.

Mom would save all her old bedding in anticipation of those long summer days and out would come boxes of sheets and blankets.

We had a clothes line in the backyard mom used to hang the washing on to dry before we got our first electric dryer. We'd throw sheets over the clothes line and stake down the corners and make pup tents to play army. When we got tired of that we'd throw sheets over fence posts and make teepee's to play Cowboys and Indians.

Once we made a circle out of some old wire fencing, threw sheets over it and made a circus underneath. I can still recall the musty smell of the old sheets as they warmed in the afternoon sun.

When we all had a tent house then we'd set out to pitch a second tent for everyone which became their imaginary place of work. We'd get paper and make signs like "Bank" or "Post Office" and stick the paper up with a wad of chewing gum and drive our bicycles and peddle tractors from tent to tent as if they were cars, trading little slips of homemade paper money to buy whatever goods the proprietor of that tent was peddling.

As a special treat sometimes we'd get to sew two blankets together and stuff them with straw to make a bed and we'd sleep out in our tents all night long.

Kids don't build tents anymore like we used to. We all grew up and went on to build all kinds of gadgets that have given the next generation a better world to live in, but now everything is made for them so they don't need to build things for themselves like we used to. They just go buy whatever they want, predesigned, prepackaged, no imagination required. Now so many of our young people fill all their days of boredom with designer drugs and other mischief. Perhaps when the art of tent making was lost they also lost a lot of lessons about the art of home building. So many homes are broken now, over five times as many as when I grew up. Perhaps its time to throw away the gadgets, bring out the old sheets and make our kids learn the art of tent building.

A Big Crowd Comes to See a Granpa Show

INTERESTING GRANPA HISTORY AND FACTS #19

Sam and Ron Badour once set up an assembly line in the shop on the Granpa home base compound and created six Granpa all metal Puppetmobiles™ in two weeks, working around the clock.

MORE STINKING RV PERMITS

- Park on the stinking beach anytime you want permit: allows the holder of the permit to park his or her recreational vehicle on any beach anytime, anywhere with or without notice and to make any other stinken place they want place into a beach any stinken time or place he or she wants to.

- Carry any stinking junk you want permit: allows the holder of the permit to carry as many lawn chairs, barbeques, mopeds, tents, weed whackers, furniture, beach supplies, tools and/or party equipment as he or she stinking well wants to.

- Drive Any Stinking Speed You Want Permit: allows the holder of the permit to drive his or her recreational vehicle any stinking speed he or she wants for the duration of whatever.

- Take Up The Whole Stinking Road Permit: allows the holder of the permit to drive his or her recreational vehicle any stinking place he or she wants for the duration of whatever.

IT ALL HAPPENED BECAUSE:

Somehow I never stopped believing who God said I was,
in spite of what life and people told me contrary.

The Misadventures of Granpa — A Major Influence

Growing up in the fifties in front of a black and white TV, Captain Kangaroo was a huge influence on me. It was my first look at puppets; Mr. Moose and Bunny Rabbit. I missed the bus the very first day of school in first grade because I had my nose stuck to the TV watching Bob Keeshan work his magic. Decades later I was standing in the lobby of the Grand Plaza hotel in Grand Rapids, Michigan where I was to M.C. a showcase. I saw this older gentleman I thought was Captain Kangaroo. I moved close and stood behind him and listened to him say a few words to someone. The moment I heard his voice I knew it was him. I introduced myself and shared how he was responsible for me missing my first day of school. I gave him a big hug and said thank you and said something to him I always wanted to say, "Can I come and be on your show?" I knew he was out of production by then, but I wanted to ask anyway. I hope that his voice to children has continued to work its magic through my voice long after he has passed. We never know who we might affect for the good, whether by the big voice of a political podium, or the small voice of a puppet on a fair ground. Perhaps I have taught a future president of the United States about the golden rule. Who knows? In any case, Bob gets a lot of the credit.

GRANPA'S RV TRIVIA

- What do you call a camper with no wheels? A drag.
- How do you know if an RV thinks he has talent? He toots his horn.
- How do you know when a RVer is a good card player? When he has a flush.
- How do you know when an RVer needs a therapist? It has a breakdown.
- What is a camper's favorite question? RV there yet?
- How do you know if an camper was just born? It's a camper with a pamper.
- What's an RVer's favorite country music song? I'm On the Road Again.

71

Granpa Agriculture Quiz #19

True or false? Agriculture is New York's largest industry.

IT ALL HAPPENED BECAUSE:

God gave me way, way, way too much energy for one person.

GRANPA'S TOP TEN DON'T DO THAT LIST FOR FOR NOVICE RVers

- Don't hug a grizzly. They tend to hug back.
- Don't sleep in poison ivy. It gives new meaning to the term "I'm itching to get outta here."
- Always carry toilet paper. The alternative is not pretty and never shake hands with a guy who is asking to borrow yours.
- When hiking leave a trail of bread crumbs. Hey, it worked for Gretel.
- Never set up your tent in quick sand. The view is restrictive.
- Don't put your bedroll down hill from the outhouse. Bleep happens, but hey, don't help it out.
- Never sleep on your leftovers. Hungry raccoons don't make good bedfellows.
- Don't' use Granma as bait. Puts her in a bad mood and when Granma's in a bad mood, everybody's in a bad mood.
- Black water does not refer to coffee. No amount of cream will help if you get it wrong.
- Read this list again – post it – memorize it – pass it on.

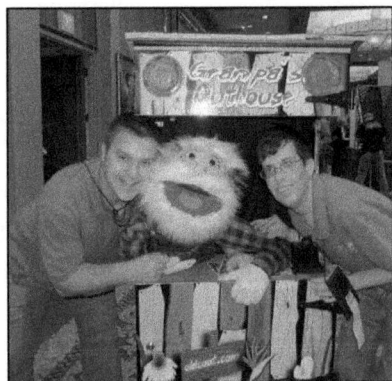

Here's Jason Fronczak and Oliver Bowman with a Granpa Puppetmobile. We've built over a dozen different mobiles for Granpa to get around in.

IT ALL HAPPENED BECAUSE:

As a kid I was given so many hours to do nothing but dream.

INTERESTING GRANPA HISTORY AND FACTS #20

Granpa has appeared on all the major networks; CBS, NBC, ABC, PBS, the Fox Network, ESPN, The LeSea Broadcasting Network, the Success in Life Network.

The Misadventures of Granpa – Granpa Gets A Hole In One

I booked the grand opening of a mall in Buffalo, New York, but only after a lot of effort convincing the mall manager that our Puppetmobile™ was perfectly safe. Upon arrival she directed me to park and set up the show trailer in a wing of the mall that didn't have any stores open yet. However, my mistake was I didn't first unload the Puppetmobile™ out of the show trailer, out in the parking lot. So, in the mall, in the narrow corridor, I let down the rear door of the trailer and went to push out the mobile by holding on the top of radiator. The mobile started down the ramp and the radiator top popped right off in my hands. The mobile rolled right down the trailer ramp and right through a newly plastered wall and disappeared out of sight. The hole in the wall was the perfect outline of the mobile; mirrors, headlights. All in wonderful detail. It was a real loony toons moment. I just stood there, stunned. When I came back to my senses I heard workers down the way so I ran down there and found a guy plastering. I paid him a hundred bucks, which was a lot of money back then, begging him to immediately come and fix the hole. He did, the show went on, and the nervous mall manager never knew it happened.

IT ALL HAPPENED BECAUSE:

Because of Bob Keeshan

Granpa Agriculture Quiz #20

True or false? Worldwide, more people eat and drink milk from goats than any other animal.

TOP TEN YOU MIGHT BE AN OLD COOT IF . . .

- Your address is a local Walmart.
- Your boot doubles as a drinking glass.
- Your house is on wheels.
- Plaid is your favorite color.
- You once traded your wife for a satellite dish.
- Your house is hooked to a truck.
- You've taken a major dump in the middle of the road, at 60 miles an hour.
- You have to put on hip waders just to flush.
- You've taken a nap at seventy five miles per hour.
- You thought tying your pet up to the back of your house was a good idea.

Granma's Show Trivia #25

What does Squirt the skunk do in some of Granpa's shows?

IT ALL HAPPENED BECAUSE:

I lost everything, then found Debbie.

The Misadventures of Granpa – A Shattering Experience

One time we had Granpa in a Puppetmobile™ entertaining and drawing traffic into a booth for a wire service at a huge flower show in a giant coliseum. Granpa had his mobile backed up to a huge wall of pottery being showcased in the booth next to us. Our performer, John Smith, swears to this day someone messed with the mobile over night and stuck the gas peddle in the full on position. He got in the mobile, turned it on and it lurched into high, reverse gear, and backed right through the wall of pottery in the booth next to us. The floors were cement and the crashing of more than a hundred clay pots was unbelievable as that whole wall came down on that cement. Everyone in the whole convention center came rushing to the booth. The disturbance was so great it literally shut down the whole convention. John called me so upset he was crying and afraid I would fire him on the spot. But, all is well that ends well. The noise and commotion got so much attention the pottery company had the biggest sales day in its history. They tried to hire Granpa to come to the next convention and run through another wall of pottery for them.

IT ALL HAPPENED BECAUSE:

A million things fell into place. Only God could orchestrate that!

INTERESTING GRANPA HISTORY AND FACTS #21

Granpa has appeared in cameos on the Today Show, Entertainment Tonight and Good Morning America.

MY DRIVING IS SO BAD . . .

A They gave me a pilots license so my right turns would be legal.

A When I took the drivers test they had to bring out the binoculars so I could take the eye exam.

🛣 My drivers test examiner made me stop at his therapist, going and coming.

🛣 My driving instructor made me drop him off at St. Judes mental ward.

🛣 The tow company has a truck meet me at every intersection.

🛣 My insurance company has a full time adjuster permanently assigned to my paperwork.

🛣 The Mayor of Sharpsville declared the first day of every month a holiday and sends everyone to the Bahamas just so I can drive into town for groceries without causing a major traffic jam.

🛣 Maude Quakenbush decided to plant cement roses so I could drive right on through her garden.

🛣 The county painted solid yellow lines on the side of the courthouse so I wouldn't try to pass between the second and third floor on my way to traffic court.

🛣 I have a permanently assigned line number at the traffic office.

Granma's Show Trivia #26

What does Fuzz Ball the dog do at the end of the general store show teaching the golden rule?

IT ALL HAPPENED BECAUSE:

I had Kimberly and Cameron to love when I had nothing else.

MY DRIVING IS SO BAD . . .

🛣 The local hospital carries three times the normal supply of casts and crutches.

🛣 They put a special question on the driver test back home just so local drivers would know how to take extreme measures in case they met me on the highway.

🛣 All the paramedic units compete for my account.

🅰 The local auto dealer is required to install my truck with the normally optional 360 degree bumper.

🅰 All my traffic tickets made my glove box explode.

🅰 They mass mail my court notices.

🅰 The police installed a permanent stop sign on my front bumper.

🅰 Rand McNally has to make road addition updates to the Sharpsville map every month.

🅰 The town removes all the fire plugs every time I drive into town.

IT ALL HAPPENED BECAUSE:

I could go on adventure with and fall in love with
my loving, gracious, heavenly Daddy.

The Misadventures of Granpa – Can't Catch a Brake

Mike Brody was an awesome entertainer. He couldn't tell you which end of a screwdriver to use, but he could play Granpa and did so for many years. One time he was entertaining at a big indoor convention somewhere and he swore the mobile got stuck in the on position. So, to get it stopped he just ran it square into a concrete pillar. That jerked his head forward and cracked it into the metal mobile frame right in front of his face and knocked him out cold. The crash made a big noise and Granpa went dead still so they called the paramedics who broke open the back door of the mobile, pried him out and carted him off on a stretcher. Mike always knew how to make a big exit.

Granma's Show Trivia #27

In the barnyard show where does the egg yoke go?

STILL MORE BAD DRIVING JOKES

A I drive where no man has driven before. Regularly

A How many towns of less than 50 people have 157 autobody repair shops?

A When they want something demolished they invite me to drive by.

A How many trucks have you ever seen with a yield sign wedged between the carburetor and the fire wall?

A How many times has your mechanic ever said, you need plugs, points and the groundhog pulled out of your carburetor.

**Granpa being arrested and towed.
Excellent publicity.**

A When my truck overheats its usually a cow wedged between the fan blade and the radiator.

A Every time I parallel park the cars in front and behind me get shorter.

A You get bugs on your windshield? I get small animals, old ladies and vinyl siding.

A You've heard of drivers being labeled high risk? They call me maximum, absolute, eternal risk.

A Most cars have an electronic voice that says, "The door is ajar. The door is ajar." Mine says, "The driver is a jerk, The driver is a jerk."

A My dealer won't sell me a new vehicle without the doors being permanently locked.

The Misadventures of Granpa – Driving Lessons

Once Mike Brody was performing at the London Fair in London, Ontario, Canada when during a show he looked out of the stage and saw the Granpa mobile driving off. He swears he had it locked up, but this ten year old kid managed to get in the mobile, figure out how to turn on the hidden switch and drive the thing off down the fairground. I figured if the kids that smart I'd hire him. He worked for me for a couple of years, till he was twelve, then he started driving a cab. Just kidding. But he did steal the mobile. One time April and Audiel Rodriquez were working the Kankakee Illinois Fair and for some reason decided to wait to load the mobile up the morning after the fair closed. They left the fairgrounds, went to their motel, and when they returned the next day the mobile was gone.

They called me in a panic, so I drove all the way over there. By the time I arrived a detective was on the scene. He walked the parameter of the fairgrounds and found tire tracks at a gate, followed them down a lane a ways and found a path knocked down in a corn field. We followed the corn path back until we came to the mobile. Someone had driven it off into a corn field, plowing down an easy to find road until it finally ran out of gas and they just walked off and left it where it was. Nothing was harmed on the mobile and even Granpa was still hanging on his hook. He wanted them arrested for kidnapping, but he couldn't remember what they looked like.

INTERESTING GRANPA HISTORY AND FACTS #21

Granpa appeared in a national PBS show, chosen because he illustrated how powerfully children can be taught by puppets.

MY DRIVING IS SO BAD . . .

- ☺ The warning lights on the dash board come on when I just look at my truck.
- ☺ Everywhere I drive there's a traffic jam because of the tow truck, the ambulance, the police car, the fire truck, the paramedics, the insurance adjuster following me around all the time.
- ☺ I keep an inflatable lawyer in my glove box.
- ☺ The government passed a law requiring me to have air bags on the side, the top and the bottom.
- ☺ I keep a landscaper on retainer.
- ☺ I have a special garage door that never closes. My garage door opener is my front fender.
- ☺ My driving teacher required a $5,000 retainer.

- ☺ The local auto store has put a limit on the gallons of body putty I can purchase per day.
- ☺ The people in Sharpsville are required to carry pedestrian insurance just so they can walk down the sidewalk.
- ☺ The local plastic surgeon stocks extra tire mark remover from the local hardware.
- ☺ My garage builder tried to sell me an airplane hanger instead, just so I'd make it through the door.
- ☺ The local air show tried to hire me as an aerobatics act.
- ☺ The local dentist keeps extra teeth in stock.
- ☺ The local counseling center keeps a psychologist on duty full time just to help the people in my town cope with my U turns.
- ☺ My license not only includes CDL (Crash Dive Landings) and motorcycle options, it also has printed on it a demolition option.
- ☺ I have my own private insurance 800 claim line.

Granpa Agriculture Quiz #21

True or false? The average dairy cow gives 200,000 glasses of milk in a lifetime.

LIKE GRANPA ALWAYS SAYS: IN HIS MOVIE EGG YOKE IN THE UNDERWEAR: DO YOUR CHORES!

The Misadventures of Granpa – A Sticky Situation

One time I was playing a Maple Syrup Festival in a little town in Ohio. It was in this little park mid town and all there was was a little maple syrup cabin and my show. They told the local police Granpa would be driving the PuppetmobileTM on the streets around the park to draw attention for the festival. Evidently one officer didn't get the memo. A police car pulled up behind me with its lights and siren turned on. The policeman came up and leaned into Granpa and said nose to nose with the puppet, real serious like, "Could I see your driver's license?"

Since I thought he was kidding I began to spout off my bad driving and police jokes like, "Hey, if you don't like the way I drive stay off the sidewalk."

"The only license I've got is for hunting and fishing."

"Whenever I see a man in blue, I say here's donuts, now let me through."

I just kept making jokes and he just kept getting redder in the face. When I didn't see any photographer after a while I thought "Oops."

We finally got it all straightened out and I didn't have to do any hard time, but it took him months to live down the snickering down at town hall. I can still see the headlines: Policeman Busts Puppet For Bad Comedy. Couldn't bring him in because he didn't have any legs. Couldn't cuff him because he only had one arm. Booked him for an infraction of code 257831, local ordinance, bad comedy presented before an official of the court. I actually feel bad for the guy. Everyone hates being made to look like a dummy, by a real "dummy."

INTERESTING GRANPA HISTORY AND FACTS #22

Granpa has appeared four times on the Today Show, twice nationally with Willard Scott and twice on the Today Show Weekend Addition in New York city.

MY DRIVING IS REALLY REALLY BAD

- Have you ever had your town permanently paint all the stop lights red?
- Have you ever had to have your mechanic remove a mailbox, a pig and a baby buggy from your radiator?
- Have you ever had your priest try to perform an exorcism on your truck?
- Have you ever had your undertaker request weekly updates on your weight and height?
- Have you ever had your doctor suggest a medical ID bracelet for your rear view mirror?
- Have you ever had your body shop take a permanent cast of your truck body?

🛣 Have you ever had the government install satellite tracking on your truck so they will know where to send the National Guard when they hear a crash.

Granpa Agriculture Quiz #22

True or false? The largest pig till date was a Poland-China hog, named 'Big Bill'. It weighed 2,552 lbs and had a height of 5 feet and a length of 9 feet.

EVEN MORE BAD DRIVING. HAVE YOUR EVER SEEN . . .

🛣 A truck specially designed by Detroit just for one customer with two completely separate sides just so telephone poles can pass cleanly down the middle?

🛣 A vehicle drag dirt and grass underneath? How about Christmas tree lights with an old lady still wrapping gifts?

🛣 The tail of a dog going in a radiator and the nose sticking out the tailpipe?

🛣 A u turn inside a parking space?

🛣 A 17 lane change? When there's only three to begin with?

🛣 A driving examiner commit harry karri?

TRIPS DOWN MEMORY LANE
WITH GRANPA CRATCHET

THE OLD TIME HUCKSTER WAGON

Lots of things have changed over the years since I was growing up back in the nineteen fifties. Now you have these huge mega grocery stores full of selves stacked with anything your pallet can imagine, shipped from all over the world. All you have to do is feast your eyes, let the fancy red laser add it all up for you and swipe your little plastic card. Ask a lot of kids today where bacon comes from and they'll say the Piggly Wiggly! But there's one thing we had when I was growing up I guarantee the kids today have never seen: a grocery store parking itself right in the drive!

PHILIPPIANS 4:4 – REJOICE IN THE LORD ALL THE TIME, NO MATTER WHAT SITUATION YOU FIND YOURSELF IN. IT OPENS THE DOOR FOR EVERYTHING HEAVEN HAS FOR YOU! (SLB TRANS)

We called our bright red rolling grocery store The Huckster Wagon. It was a hybrid of school bus, delivery truck and gypsy wagon, ran by Virgil Carter out of his grocery store in Sharpsville. His Huckster Wagon had a narrow aisle down the middle with goods stacked from the floor to the ceiling. I can still remember the smell of the aged wood and hear the clicking of the old hand crank adding machine. He'd stack your groceries in a cardboard box and carry it inside for you if you needed him to and he'd often stock exactly what he knew you'd be needing. I'd often take a hand full of coins and buy Bazooka Bubble Gum, realistic looking candy cigarettes, or a miniature six pack of colored juice in paraffin coke bottles.

Now you can get on the computer and order anything you want and it'll show up in a brown truck in a day or two. It's really convenient, but I know I'm just x's and o's somewhere on a hard drive. I know there's no way I'll ever see a computer park itself in my drive and chat with me about what's going on in the neighborhood while it stocks a box full of goodies. Now we connect more than ever electronically, but I'm afraid we really know people less than ever. While Virgil mainly delivered groceries I think he actually delivered what people really needed most and still do; connection to a caring neighbor who lives, works and raises family in our neighborhood with our old fashioned ideas about what is right and good.

I have spent my life as Granpa Cratchet delivering stories from the good old days to kids at local fairs and I know this one thing is true; you and I are just like Virgil's rolling huckster wagon. We are stoked full of wonderful stories from the good old days and every time we drive to the homes of our great grandchildren and deliver some of those stories to them from our past we do just like Virgil did, we deliver to them what really counts - the values and heritage that is packaged inside our wonderful stories from the good ole days.

INTERESTING GRANPA HISTORY AND FACTS #23

Granpa's first national TV appearance came when he appeared with Dick VanPatten and Barbara Mandrel in A Day at the Fair, produced at the Heart of Illinois Fair, which aired in primetime on the CBS television network.

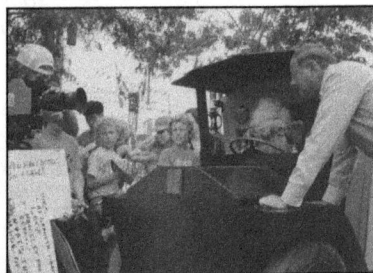

Granpa on CBS with Dick VanPatten

STILL MORE BAD DRIVING . . .

- Do you think anyone really notices my bad driving?
- Where do you think John Deere got the idea for the breaking plow?
- Where do you think Caterpillar got the idea for the earth mover?
- Where do you think Nobel got the idea for dynamite?
- Where do you think Truman got the idea for dropping the bomb?
- Who do you think was really at the wheel of the Titanic?
- Who do you think they tried to pin that Hindenburg thing on?

INTERESTING GRANPA HISTORY AND FACTS #24

Granpa was awarded best grounds act entertainment by the Oklahoma State Fair.

The Misadventures of Granpa – I Really Got Their Goat

This one time John Smith was out at a fair, where kids often show their animals; cows, pigs, rabbits and goats. This kid was out walking his miniature goat when Granpa came along in his mobile. He wanted to shake hands and talk so he tied the goat to the back of the mobile and came around front to talk to Granpa. I can hear you thinking, "Oh, no." Yep. He got caught up in it all and forgot the goat. John eventually decided to drive on across the fairgrounds, but didn't know about the goat tied on back and evidently his little legs couldn't keep up. People kept yelling, "Granpa, you're dragging a goat!" Granpa kept making jokes about the old goat called Granma. He thought they were teasing so he just kept driving on. Eventually someone hailed him down and got him to stop and explained he really was dragging a goat. The poor thing was all dusty, panting and worn out, but none the worse for the wear. People often get my goat, but that was one time I guess we got someone else's goat for a change. The incident was the talk of the fair for the rest of the week. Anything for a little publicity. Anyway, the incident won Granpa a first place trophy in 4-H goat showmanship.

HOW MANY DRIVERS DO YOU KNOW . . .

- ☹ Have their own cemetery dedicated exclusively for their victims?
- ☹ Have been featured on America's most wanted just for their parallel parking?
- ☹ Have their picture up in the post office just because they get up every day and start their truck?
- ☹ Have the whole east parking lot of the mall roped off just so they can parallel park?

OUTHOUSE JOKES

- 🧻 My motorized outhouse gives new meaning to the phrase, "You can't take it with you."
- 🧻 Back in my day high speed access meant an outhouse without a door.

- The jobs not over till the paper works done.
- You might be an old coot if you wish your bathroom in the house was as nice as your outhouse.
- I hate to flush and run but ...
- She's a two seat'r, care to join me?
- You know why blond's (insert the name of your team's favorite rival) don't use outhouses? They keep getting their head stuck in the hole.
- Sears and Roebuck made a fortune mass mailing catalogues to finer, upscale outhouses.

INTERESTING GRANPA HISTORY AND FACTS #25

Granpa was awarded best local commercial by the Illinois Association of Broadcasters for commercials created for Shields Auto Center.

GRANPA ON DATING

- I went with a bag date once. She was so ugly you had to put a bag over her head.
- I once went out with a double bagger. A girl so ugly you had to put a bag over her head and one over yours in case hers blew off.
- When I was young I had a long list of requirements for the right woman. The older I got the shorter the list got. Now I only have one requirement, she has to be breathing.
- I'm so desperate I get up in the morning and check the obituaries, go down to the funeral home and check for pulses. Hey, they make mistakes. Sometimes she's just in a deep sleep. You never know at our age. Anyway, if she has a pulse I ask her out. Sometimes that means I just take her out of embalming. Sometimes we don't make it as far as the front door before the date is over, if you know what I mean.
- The best think about mortuary dating is at least you know you'll rarely get a turn down.

The Misadventures of Granpa – I Don't See No Blood!

Our first Puppetmobiles™ were made of wood in our shop and fit cross ways, out in the open, on the front of a flat bed trailer. One time I was driving to the San Antonio Livestock show and about mid afternoon the mobile came unstrapped and rolled off the trailer, on the passenger side, and hit the ground sideways while I was driving sixty miles an hour down the interstate. As soon as it hit the ground the momentum made it roll. It must have done twenty flips and flew into a thousand pieces, wood, batteries, wires, tires, decorations flying all over. In my review mirror it looked like a sideways tornado. When I got back to the scene some old guy was picking through the debris saying, "I don't see no blood. I don't see no blood." He thought a real car had wrecked. I tried to explain what a Puppetmobile was, but he couldn't get it. He kept saying, "I don't see no blood." I picked up all those pieces, stacked them on the trailer, drove all the way through, arrived in San Antonio about three in the morning, screwed all the pieces back together, rewired the whole thing and appeared in their eleven a.m. opening parade, as scheduled. That's called gumption.

GRANPA'S LATEST STOCK MARKET INVESTMENTS

- ✗ Electric Mosquito Fence (Hey, it works for cows doesn't it?)
- ✗ Salted Band-Aids (Designed to help you forget the real injury.)
- ✗ Aerosol Tire Deflator (So you have your flat where you want it, at your convenience.)
- ✗ Skunk After Shave (So you don't have to put up with all those pesky invitations from gorgeous women.)
- ✗ Chicken Dentures (They have cavities too, you know.)
- ✗ Cement Bobbers (For men who like to sleep more than fish.)
- ✗ Bald Sports for Men
- ✗ Screen Doors for Submarines
- ✗ Glassless Windows (No streaks to bother cleaning.)
- ✗ Half Price Up Only Airline Tickets (No down side to this one.)

- #10 Grit Toilet Paper (Cuts number of trips to bathroom way down.)
- Electric Toilet Paper
- Rubber Nails
- Cement Pillows
- Square Tires (Don't wear out as often, cause you don't tend to go as far.)
- Stickless Glue (No clean up here.)
- Cement Life Jacket (For mean mother-in-laws, mean bankers and tax collectors.)
- Porcelain Hammers
- Nose Picker Attachment for Electric Drills
- Do It Yourself Heart Bypass Kit (Not for the faint of heart.)

INTERESTING GRANPA HISTORY AND FACTS #26

Granpa was awarded a national merit of mention by the National Auto Dealers Association for his auto commercials.

The Misadventures of Granpa – Granpa's Most Embarrassing Moment

I have been called a lot of things by kids over time: Granpa Hatchet, Granpa Smash-it, Shotgun Red, Granpa Hacker, Uncle Granpa, Granpa Cracker. But the worst is what I called myself once. I went on a local TV talk show and when the host asked me to introduce myself I tripped over my words and what should have come out as Granpa Cratchet came out sounding like Granpa Crapshit (Sorry about my French, but I just couldn't tell this without saying what I really said). We both started to snicker and then laugh

WEEK early morning show, but not the one where Granpa called himself a really nasty name.

88

and we just couldn't stop. That was pretty much the end of the interview. We just sat there and laughed for five straight minutes. Still to this day, when I really need to laugh, I think of this moment in my life. A couple months back my wife punched me in the middle of the night and asked me what I was laughing at. Granpa has appeared on hundreds of local TV shows promoting local events. He's always a big hit. Interviewers love him because he's so energetic. They're used to slow, boring people who come on to show their rock collections or explain in detail all the ins and outs (Pun intended) of a rectal exam.

Granpa Agriculture Quiz #23

True or false? Cows like to buffet. They eat for eight hours a day and consume over 40 pounds of food.

USED TO BE . . .

- ◀◀ Used to be bailout meant your plane was going down.
- ◀◀ Used to be bailout meant your boat had a hole in it.
- ◀◀ Used to be when someone yelled bailout it meant you had to duck 'cause a bail of straw was coming out of the barn.
- ◀◀ Used to be bailout meant you had to go down to the jail and pay to get Granma out so she could come home and cook supper.
- ◀◀ Used to be a remote meant a secluded spot off the beaten path.
- ◀◀ Used to be cable was something you used to pull your truck out of the mud.
- ◀◀ Used to be a video game was trying to make out what the fuzzy images were on a snowy black and white 10 inch screen.
- ◀◀ Used to be a cell phone was what Granma used to make her one phone call from the county jail.
- ◀◀ Used to be a calculator was the accountant who did your taxes.
- ◀◀ Used to be an airbag was some guy who talked too much.
- ◀◀ Used to be digital computing was actually counting on your digits.
- ◀◀ Used to be high speed access was an on-ramp to the freeway.
- ◀◀ Used to be high speed access was an outhouse that didn't have a door on it.

- Used to be surfing was something done on a board on the water.
- Used to be a birthday was something you actually looked forward to.

INTERESTING GRANPA HISTORY AND FACTS #27

Sam was named entrepreneur of the year by the Tipton Economic Development Commission.

BAD CHICKEN TRIVIA (Great for kids age five and under)

- Why do chickens live in hen houses? (Because they can't afford condos!)
- How much does a pound of feathers weigh? (Blonds never get this one!)
- What does it mean if you say someone gets up with the chickens? (They get up early, not that they slept with the chickens.)
- When is chicken soup bad for you? (When you're the chicken!)

THIS WEEK'S GRANPA'S GENERAL STORE COUPON PROMOTION

This week Granpa's General Store is featuring Granpa's Do It Yourself Heart Bypass Kits, at 70% off normal retail price, with coupon from the Homegrown Gazette. The kit includes everything you need; saw, hammer, chisel, scoop shovel, garden hose, a refurbed hand cranked oil pump (Battery powered pump extra), and smelling salts to assure you stay fully awake during the operation. Instruction book available for an extra fee. You also get a 2% off coupon from the U.R. Gruesome Mortuary and Bowling Alley located in downtown Sharpsville, since you have about a 2% chance of survival. With U.R. Gruesome you can roll a strike or you can strike out, either way you win.

The Misadventures of Granpa – Granpa's Biggest Laugh

The biggest laugh I ever got in my forty years of show business was at a little fair down in southern Illinois. They asked me if I would appear at their tractor pull. So I wrote a cute little skit centered around the way we used to have tractor pulls back in the early days when they simply hooked a big sheet of metal behind a tractor and people would hop on as the tractor drove by. As the night would wear on people would get tired and go home and they would have to get anyone to hop on the sled they could, so they would end up with people of all ages and sizes. So I found this real little kid and this huge, seven foot tall, four hundred pound farmer and roped a sheet of plywood to the back of the Puppetmobile. The idea was to bog down when the big guy got on my sled and do a lot of complaining and hope for some smiles. In front of a packed grandstand that night I took off pulling my sled and I saw the little kid pass by on my right, then I saw the big farmer as I passed him, but I couldn't see when they got on the sled back behind me. So, I just took a shot in the dark.

PHILIPPIANS 4:6 – DON'T WORRY ABOUT A DAG GONE THING. ITS PRAYER THAT CHANGES THINGS. BUT WHEN YOU PRAY MIX IN BEING THANKFUL FOR WHAT HE HAS DONE AND WHAT HE WILL DO (SLB TRANS)

When the big farmer passed by, I hit the brake as hard as I could and slammed Granpa up onto the windshield, hoping for a laugh. At that moment thirty thousand people in the grandstands erupted into huge, roaring laughter and a standing ovation. Later I asked what had happened. Evidently the big farmer never even got to hop on my sled. I had hit the brake at the exact moment he had simply laid his right foot on the edge of the sled. It probably helped that everyone in the county knew the big guy and he was the nicest person you'd ever want to meet. Anyway, it once again proves true the old entertainment axiom; the key to comedy is - timing.

IT ALL HAPPENED BECAUSE:

Because God knew Anthony would come into my life and I would need all this stuff to share with him so he would know the awesome God I know and know that He will do the same thing for him He did for me.

INTERESTING GRANPA HISTORY FACT #28

The largest live crowd Granpa ever appeared in front of was a Puppetmobile™ appearance in front of sixty thousand plus, at an ESPN monster truck pull, at the coliseum in Indianapolis Indiana.

PIG JOKES

- What do you give a pig with a rash? Oinkment.
- What do you say when your pet pig tells a tall story? That's hog wash .
- Why couldn't the pig get a date? He was a boar.
- What's a pig's favorite quick mart? The Stop And Slop.
- What is a pig's favorite way to gamble? A slop machine.
- What do you call a pig with no legs? A ground hog.
- How do you call a pig without legs? You don't. He won't come anyway.
- What do you call it when celebrities get together at a banquet and tell jokes about their favorite pig? A hog roast.
- What's a hog's favorite fragrance? Pigpourri.
- What's a hog's favorite ice cream? Pigstachio.

INTERESTING GRANPA HISTORY AND FACTS #29

Most of the puppets are purchased from suppliers, but Granpa is made one at a time, by hand, in the puppet birthing center by Sam. The most ever paid for a puppet was seven thousand dollars, for an animatronic Granpa puppet used in high profile media appearances.

IT ALL HAPPENED BECAUSE:

I could write all my books for you, to encourage you and help you, so you might do great and mighty things for God's kingdom.

MORE BAD PIG JOKES

- What is a pig's favorite karate move? The pork chop.
- What do you call a crafty pig? A cunning-ham.
- Why did the pig throw a party? So he could go hog wild.
- What do you call the story of the 3 little pigs? A pig tale.
- What's pig's favorite form of transportation? Pig Up Trucks.
- Where do bad pigs go? To the pigpen-itentiary.
- Why aren't pigs good at playing tug of war? Pigs want to go into the mud.
- Why didn't the pigs listen to their teacher? He was a boar.
- Why are pigs great football fans? They are always rooting.
- How do you take a pig to the hospital? In a ham-bulance.
- What do you call a pig with no money? A poor boar.
- Why do pigs make good carpenters? They love to boar holes.
- Where do Chinese pigs live? Singaboar.
- Where are the presidential pig's faces carved? In Mount Rushboar.

TRIPS DOWN MEMORY LANE
WITH GRANPA CRATCHET

THE OLD GENERAL STORE

I spent a lot of hours following my mom's skirt tails in the old general stores around the area where I lived as a child. Every old store had a personality all its own and if you hung around them very often you began to feel like you were visiting an old friend.

There was an old general store at the crossroads about a mile or so from our house at Prairie Corners. It had a case of meats at one end, some shelves on two of the walls with basic food items and that was about it. There were a few chairs scattered around an old pot belly stove in the center of the room. There wasn't ever really any reason to stop in for anything because they weren't going to have it anyway so you'd stop in just to pick up the warm feeling that someone was glad to see you.

A few miles away in Sharpsville was Carter's General Store. It had stuff piled high and as you walked through the store from one end to another you could tell where you were in the store just by seeing with your nose. From aisle to aisle you could tell if you were in front of the cereal, the overalls or the meats. For just a moment or two you could lose all your troubles in a mental trip to paradise while strolling down an aisle stocked full of freshly picked peaches.

MATTHEW 6:27 – THERE IS NOT ONE PERSON ON EARTH WHO HAS THE POWER TO MAKE HIS LIFE ANY BETTER BY WORRYING. (SLB TRANS)

Across the street was the Sharpsville grain elevator where we took corn and wheat to sell or be ground into feed. It had its own unique blend of odors that said commerce-takes-place-here. You could have blindfolded me, drove me around for hours and then walked me into that store and I would have known immediately where I was. The smell of the feeds, the dog food, the grain and the odor of cut woods that drifted in from the lumber yard connected to the back gave that store its own special aroma personality and when you stepped into it you knew it was the center for farming commerce.

We did a lot of our grocery shopping in another little town close by called Russiaville, in a store called Martin's. It was an old building, with creaky wooden floors. Almost every step you took down every aisle was answered by a creak or a pop or a groan, as if you were walking down the spine of an old man that made his age known by moaning every step you took as you moved from where you picked up your shopping basket at his toes till you checked out at the big old cash register at the tip of his nose. Those old wooden floors had soaked up every kind of product and every kind of juice from over a half century of spills and gave off a scent that would make any candlemaker melt with envy.

I remember my Grandma Bowman worked at Chews' Grocery over in Burlington. Like most of the stores it's walls looked like aged wood that had never been painted and had aged over the years to a weathered General Store grey both inside and out. Now those old wooden slates were like memory chips that had filled up with all the smells of fresh cut meats and powdered sugar, potatoes and fruit and veggies which had made their way in and out the front door for decades. What made Chews' special was that they didn't allow anyone behind the front counter. You had to hand them your list and wait while they gathered all the items for you. I often wondered as a little kid if this was because all those things on all those shelves were too precious for us common folk to see and touch on our own. My own Grandma Bowman was special, because she wore a white apron and could go behind the counter and touch all those wonderful things.

On the other hand, Compton's General Store, which still operates down in the county seat of Tipton is more of a hardware store with smells of oils and old machinery. The windows are still filled with baskets, old wash tubs, buckets, coal oil lamps and hand pumps. The store looks totally disorganized, but the proprietor knows exactly where every item is by memory. You can tell how long something has been there by the dates people have written in the dust that coats that item and when you check out he rounds everything to the lowest dollar so he doesn't have to mess with change. If you need to keep the flies out or the chickens in, Compton's Hardware is the place you go.

Most of those stores are gone now, replaced by huge, megastores in the big city. They put people at the front door to make you think you're meeting an old friend when you enter, but they don't fool me. None of them know my name, my dog's name, my mom's name or her mom's name or really care about how Aunt Myrtle's gout is doing. I know because every time I try to talk to them about it they get this far away look in their eyes. The place smells like cleaners and electronics and sweaty people busy pushing big carts and racing in and out of parking places to hurry off to somewhere else they really don't need to go.

If I could make any change to our country right now it would be to require every store to be small enough for me to hear the owner's answer if I call out a question. Every floor would be required to creak and it would be mandatory for every store to have their own patented odor. Every proprietor would be required to know three things; my name, my family history back at least two generations and all the latest news from the farm next door.

INTERESTING GRANPA HISTORY AND FACTS #30

Sam played Seaweed Sam and performed a host of puppets and costume characters, and appeared with Granpa, on more than seventy five episodes of the Captain Hook Show, broadcast nationally on twenty three over the air stations and on more than 120 cable outlets.

Granpa Agriculture Quiz #24

True or false? Insulin and about 40 other medicines are made from pigs.

MORE STUPID PIG JOKES

- What do you call it when a pig takes a long drink of cola? A pig-swig.
- What's a hog's favorite indoor game? Pig-pong.
- What do you call a funny pig? A ham.
- What is a pig doing when he's putting something in the oven? He's bacon.
- What kind of a motorcycle does a pig ride? A hog.
- How can you tell if a pig has a boyfriend? She has a ring in her nose.
- Where does a pig do his laundry? At the hog wash.
- What do you get when you cross a pig with a canary? Don't know, but if it sits on your electric wire the lights go out.
- Why don't you tell a pig your secrets? Becasue he'll always squeal.
- Why is a pig like a penny? It's head is on one side and its tail is on the other.
- Why do pigs always buy four-wheel drive trucks? They're always stuck in the mud.
- What famous pig did King Aurthor knight? Sir Lunchalot.
- What did the pig say when the wolf grabbed her tail? That's the end of me.
- What world famous pig athletic event is held every four years? The Olympigs.
- What did the boy pig send the girl pig on February 14th? A Valenswine.
- Who's the greatest hog painter of all time? Pigcasso.

The Misadventures of Granpa – Don't Lose Your Head

We make our Grandpa puppets in our shop. We've gone through many designs and improvements over the years. We made some out of latex for a while and sewed the neck to the body. Evidently I made the stitches too small and it made a perforation effect around the neck. While performing Granpa's head popped right off the body. The body fell down my arm out of sight. All the audience could see was Granpa's head on the end of my arm. I finished the show with a nude Granpa and nobody noticed, or at least nobody said anything.

INTERESTING GRANPA HISTORY FACT #31

Granpa's first Puppetmobile™ was called a huckster wagon because it was fashioned after a real delivery truck people called a huckster wagon. Virgil Carter made the circuit in our county from Carter's General Store in Sharpsville selling groceries.

GRANPA DATES A MANNEQUIN

These are jokes Granpa used in his Granpa Dates Ashley video. We put Granpa with a mannequin at the Florida Strawberry festival and let him talk about Ashley, his special date. This is a record for the most one liners Granpa ever told in one sitting. You can watch it on YouTube.

- ✗ Her name is Ashley Mannequin.
- ✗ She models clothing in store windows.
- ✗ Instead of going to Mary Kay parties she goes to Wood Putty Parties.
- ✗ She doesn't walk she lumbers.

MATTHEW 6:30 – IF GOD CAN SET UP THIS WHOLE WORLD AND FIGURE OUT HOW TO TAKE CARE OF EVERY LITTLE LIVING THING IN IT, DO YOU THINK HE WILL LEAVE YOU OUT? NEVER! SO, SHOW A LITTLE FAITH THE NEXT TIME YOU'RE TEMPTED TO WORRY OVER SOMETHING. (SLB TRANS)

✘ Every time she goes to sit down she yells timber.

✘ Favorite singing group is The Carpenters.

✘ Eats like she's got a hollow leg. I took it off and looked. Yep. Totally hollow.

✘ She sleeps like a log. Snores like a chainsaw.

✘ Took her for a picnic and the ants paid more attention to her than the food.

✘ She pines for love.

✘ She doesn't say much, but she doesn't talk back either.

✘ She was offered a job at the post office, holding up a mail box.

✘ Her brother's a kitchen cabinet in Sacramento.

✘ Every time I kiss her goodnight I have to pull the splinters out of my lips. We never French kiss, its just way too painful.

✘ She a little conservative, I'm trying to get her to branch out.

✘ Only way to tell how old she is is to cut her in half and count her rings.

✘ When she has a cavity she makes an appointment with a drill press.

✘ She doesn't have any arthritis, but she has lots of trouble with stiff joints.

✘ Her mom was a maple tree and her dad was a chainsaw.

✘ I took her out for a drink and she got nailed.

✘ Whenever I take her into Home Depot she keeps wandering toward the power sanders.

✘ She's still trying to get over her break up with her last boyfriend; a surfboard.

INTERESTING GRANPA HISTORY FACT #32

All the granpa shows are set up and performed by one person, contain as many as fifteen puppets, and can have up to one hundred entrances and exits in each show.

MORE ASHLEY MANNEQUIN JOKES

- ✕ She once fell in love with a nail gun.
- ✕ Most people think she's stuck up, but she's really just shy.
- ✕ She applies her makeup with a caulk gun.
- ✕ She's real sad, her best friend just got turned into barn siding.
- ✕ She's deathly afraid of wood chippers.
- ✕ She asked me to go out with her and I said "Wood I!" She thought I was calling her names and slapped me.
- ✕ She volunteers downtown as a shelter for homeless squirrels.
- ✕ She wanted me to give her a rub down, said she had a knot in her neck.
- ✕ For Valentine's day I bought her a book: "Falling in love for dummies".
- ✕ I asked her to give me her hand in marriage and she did, along with her forearm, elbow and shoulder.
- ✕ She's very stiff and inflexible. I think she just might be a republican.
- ✕ She looks really thin, but she retains water.
- ✕ She can be a real hard head.
- ✕ She's real nice but she can also be real knotty. Get it? Knotty (as in naughty?).
- ✕ Her family roots go back to some of the best storm drains and sewer tiles.
- ✕ I asked her to go for a walk in the woods and she got attacked by a clan of beavers. Chewed her legs right off and made this really nice dam.

Ashley Mannequin

INTERESTING GRANPA HISTORY FACT #33

The most individual sales Granpa ever made in one day was at The Sandwich Fair, Sandwich, Illinois. It was on a Saturday at their one hundred and fiftieth anniversary. One thousand two hundred kids lined up over the course of nine hours to buy a $1 poster from Granpa at the front door of Granpa's Barnyard. At the end of the day I had to pry my fingers out of the puppet.

The Misadventures of Granpa – On Getting a Smooch From A Fair Queen

One time I was M.C. of the talent showcase at the West Virginia Association of Fairs convention. There were about a thousand people in the audience. As a fun routine I decided I would interview the West

Not the queen that fell behind the desk.

Virginia Fair Queen between showcasing music groups. She comes out totally dressed in a lavish evening gown, high heels and beautiful golden hair piled high on her head, topped with a jeweled crown. I ask fun, embarrassing questions about dating and get lots of laughs. At the end of the skit I ask the fair queen for a little peck on the cheek, then just as she turns to give Granpa the kiss I turn his head so her kiss lands right on his lips. This got a huge laugh so I got a little too excited and carried it a little to far.

I made some comment about her being out of practice, which got a laugh, so I asked her for another one so I could show her how it's really done. Being good natured she played along and as she leaned over I placed my left hand behind her neck and put her in a big lip lock by putting Granpa's whole mouth over her whole face. I began making huge sucking sounds and swaying her back and forth. She got turned around in her seat, lost her balance, fell off her chair, right into my lap and out of sight behind my interview desk. Granpa came up huffing and puffing, she came up with her

100

hair all fallen down over her face and her crown missing. The crowd fell out of their seats. I didn't have to tell one more joke the rest of the night. Every time the spot light came back on me I just kept saying "I am so sorry" and the crowd started laughing all over again, a true comedy moment in my life as Granpa.

TOMBSTONES YOU'LL ONLY SEE IN THE GRANPA'S HOME TOWN CEMETERY

- GONE AND FORGOTTEN
- HATES ANIMALS, HATED KIDS - GLAD HE'S GONE
- HERE LIES HAROLD – SHOT BY HIS FOURTH WIFE R.I.P.
- LOVING WIFE – MOTHER – CONSUMER SHOPPED TILL SHE DROPPED
- HERE LIES GRANPA BLAKE - STEPPED ON THE GAS INSTEAD OF THE BRAKE
- I'D RATHER BE HERE THAN WITH HER
- HERE LIES WILLIAM BLAKE - WAS HANGED BY MISTAKE
- HERE LIES ZEKE - SECOND FASTEST DRAW IN CRIPPLE CREEK
- NOW WHERE DID I PUT THAT ANTIDOTE?
- SHE ALWAYS WANTED TO SEE HOW A GUN WORKED
- HERE LIES EMILY WHITE - SHE SIGNALED LEFT AND THEN TURNED RIGHT
- HERE'S MY WIFE MUCH LAMENTED - NOW SHE'S HAPPY AND I'M CONTENTED
- HERE LIES THE TOWN BANKER - HIS FINAL VAULT
- HERE LIES A POLITICIAN - STILL DOING WHAT HE DOES BEST
- His kids put this on the tombstone of Orville Redenbacher: HERE LIES POP - HE WAS BURIED IN EXTRA BUTTER

JOSHUA 1:6 – BE STRONG AND HAVE A LOT OF COURAGE BECAUSE I WILL GIVE YOU EVERYTHING YOU NEED, AS AN INHERITANCE, SIMPLY BECAUSE YOU ARE MY SON OR DAUGHTER! (SLB TRANS)

- ☠ HERE LIES THE TOWN MORTICIAN
- ☠ HE WHO FILLS THIS TOMB HELPED FILL THIS CEMETERY
- ☠ HERE LIES THE TOWN DENTIST - FILLING HIS LAST CAVITY
- ☠ HERE LIES THE BANK ROBBER - HE'S LYING LOW FOR A WHILE
- ☠ HERE LIES CARL THE PLUMBER - HE TOOK HIS FINAL PLUNGE
- ☠ HERE LIES THE TOWN WRITER - HIS FINAL PLOT
- ☠ HERE LIES THE TOWN INVESTOR - HE WENT IN THE HOLE ON THIS ONE
- ☠ HERE LIES THE TOWN GAMBLER - HE CASHED IN HIS CHIPS
- ☠ HERE LIES THE TOWN UNDERTAKER
- ☠ LET US REJOICE - IF HE HAD LIVED HE WOULD HAVE BURIED US ALL
- ☠ HERE LIES THE TOWN ATHIEST - ALL DRESSED UP AND NO PLACE TO GO
- ☠ On the tomb of the town hypochondriac : I TOLD YOU I WAS SICK

INTERESTING GRANPA HISTORY FACT #34

Granpa has met many world famous actors, country singers, many governors and senators, and three presidents of the United States, and some really important people, too.

The Misadventures of Granpa – Pecking Order, Or Pecking Out of Order

John Smith tells about performing the chicken show one time in which the kids were yelling at Granpa to help him catch the chicken. When Granpa had caught his chicken the kids kept right on yelling about catching the chicken! Evidently a real rooster got out of his cage and was running loose all through the audience flopping and pecking kids and everyone was yelling

"Catch the chicken!" We're still not sure if the rooster just got loose or some wisenheimer threw him into the crowd on purpose.

GRANPA PHONE PRANKS

(RING Hey, is your refrigerator running right now? I think so. Well then you better go catch it! CLICK

(RING Is boo there. Boo who? Oh, quit your whinning you big baby!! CLICK

(RING Is Jimmy there? Jimmy who? Jimmy five bucks and I'll quit calling! CLICK

(RING Yanita. Yanita who. You Yanita Bath, I can smell you long distance. CLICK

(RING Oliver. Oliver who, Don't look now but Oliver Clothes are off! CLICK

(RING Lettuce. Lettuce who. Don't look, the lettuce is dressing. CLICK

(RING Jacque. Jacque who? Jacque Itch, so you better scratch! CLICK

(RING Heywood. Heywood who? Heywould you send me some money? I need a new pacemaker! CLICK

(RING Cuddle. Cuddle who? Me you big dope, I'm lonely. CLICK

INTERESTING GRANPA HISTORY AND FACTS #35

Granpa once addressed a meeting of the general public along with the governor of the State of Michigan at the Ionia Free Fair, in Ionia, Michigan.

Jimmy, Sam and Jason building Granpas

The Misadventures of Granpa – On Hiring Mic Baylor

Mic Baylor was, hands down, the funniest person I ever met. Everything that came out of the man's mouth was a joke, 24/7. I am not kidding and it was all funny. He grew up in Detroit, Michigan, which explains a lot about Mic. I asked him several times to write me some jokes and he never did, because if you asked him to be funny he couldn't think of a thing to say. So much of his humor was situational that it couldn't be captured and repeated. He had an awesome wit and was perfect for Puppetmobile™ improv. I first met him when he came to where I was working one night fixing something under a Puppetmobile™.

He grabbed a puppet off a table and stuck it under the mobile and started making jokes about my welding. I started laughing and I asked him if he was available for the summer. His puppet snuggled up to me and said in a Groucho Marx sort of way, "No, but I'll dump my girlfriend on labor day and you can have me as many times as you want in the fall." I said you're hired without ever seeing his face. Good thing. Anyway, Mic is one of my best success stories. Not only was Granpa his ticket out of Detroit, he wanted to be a cartoonist and was very talented. So he worked for me all summer to pay his way through art college in the winter. He has now worked for the big boys like Disney and Sony, among others.

YOU KNOW YOU'RE OLD WHEN

- ✗ You know you're old when your back goes out more times than you do.
- ✗ When you make dirt look young.
- ✗ You can remember the big bang.
- ✗ Everything hurts and what doesn't hurt, doesn't work.
- ✗ The gleam in your eye is from the sun hitting your bifocals.
- ✗ You feel like the night before and you haven't been anywhere.
- ✗ Your little black book contains only names ending in M.D.
- ✗ You get winded playing checkers.
- ✗ Your children begin to look old.
- ✗ You join a health club and don't go.

✗ You decide to procrastinate but never get around to it.

✗ You know you used to chase women, but can't remember why.

✗ A dripping faucet causes a bladder urge.

✗ You look forward to a dull evening.

✗ You walk with your head held high just to get used to your bifocals.

INTERESTING GRANPA HISTORY FACT #36

The longest puppet show Sam ever performed was when he was M.C. for the Michigan Association of Fairs, at the Amway Grand Plaza Hotel, in Grand Rapids, Michigan, about 1988. He put on a full body puppet at about 6:15 p.m. and didn't stop until after twelve acts had showcased, and the people had all filed out of the auditorium, just before midnight. He puppeteered before a live audience for almost five straight hours. It took five days to work out hand cramps.

MORE YOU KNOW YOU'RE OLD WHEN JOKES

✗ Your favorite column in the newspaper is 50 Years Ago Today.

✗ You turn out the lights for economic reasons rather than romantic reasons.

✗ You sit in a rocking chair but can't get started.

✗ Your knees buckle but your belt won't.

✗ You regret all the times you resisted temptation.

✗ Dialing long distance wears you out.

✗ You can't stand people who are intolerant.

ISAIAH 61:7 – IF WHILE YOU ARE ACTIVELY TRUSTING AND WORKING FOR ME YOU SUFFER LOSS, THEN I MYSELF WILL GIVE YOU DOUBLE FOR YOUR LOSSES. (SLB TRANS)

✗ The best part of your day is over when the alarm goes off in the morning.

✗ You burn out your midnight oil before 8 pm.

✗ When a pretty girl goes by your pacemaker makes the garage door go up.

✗ The little old lady you help across the street is your wife.

✗ You have too much room in your house and not enough room in your medicine cabinet.

✗ You sink your teeth into a steak and they stay there.

✗ Some lady said she was around 40. I took one look at her and said, ya, the second time around.

✗ When your body is worth a fortune. Silver in your hair, gold in your teeth, stones in your kidneys, lead in your feet and gas in your stomach.

✗ Your friends are old. You wake up with Will Power, you have to immediately go and see John, Charlie Horse stays all morning, Authur Ritis stays all afternoon, and you go to bed with Ben Gay in the evening.

Granpa Agriculture Quiz #25

True or false? A pumpkin is 90% water.

The Misadventures of Granpa – One Way to Meet Chicks

Adiel Rodriquez was about the nicest guy you would ever want to meet, so I hired him to perform Granpa. At one of his gigs, the Iowa State Fair, he bumped into a beautiful young lady with the Puppetmobile™ and knocked her down. He hopped out to see if she was alright, they fell in love and were married a year later on that very spot, on the fairground. She is quite cute and he never ran into anything else, so I'm not sure about his claim that the accident was an accident.

WHAT DO YOU CALL . . .

⇒ A cow with no legs? Ground beef.

⇒ A pig with no legs? A ground hog.

⇒ A dog with no legs? Nothing, he won't come anyway.

⇒ A frog with no legs? A low toad.

⇒ A goose with no legs? A sitting duck?

⇒ A supermodel with no legs? Out of work.

⇒ A chair with no legs? Firewood.

⇒ A table with 5 legs? Poor craftsmanship.

INTERESTING GRANPA HISTORY AND FACTS #37

From 1995 to present most tours have been four units. In 2012 old equipment was retired and two units refurbished which remain on the road to this day.

The Misadventures of Granpa – A Free Meal

One of our Granpa performers, Chris Rafinski, could be the most anal about details of any creative, performer type person I ever met. One moment he would be harping on some detail he had listed in his notebook and the next moment he'd be the funniest, carefree person you could ever meet. One time we went into a Bob Evans restaurant to eat and there were about thirty people crowded into a tiny area waiting to be seated. They had this podium which had a microphone they used to call out names when people's table was ready. People were getting testy and Chris was getting bored so he steps up to the microphone and starts telling jokes. Pretty soon everyone is laughing and having a grand time. Finally he picks up the list of names and says, "Oh – attention everyone, attention everyone. All your tables are now ready" to which he gets a huge round of applause. We did finally get our table and when it came time to pay his meal was free. Someone had paid for his plate.

GRANPA'S NEW FARM SCENTED AFTERSHAVES

- Pigpourri: A mild, earthy aroma with a hint of dirt and fresh rain.
- Suddenly Sheep: Makes you want to cuddle up with something soft, that bleats.
- Heavenly Hog: Smells like nothing on earth - you'd want to smell.
- Days of Swine and Roses: Ah, the memories.
- Uncommonly Cow: Has a rich smooth, mellow moo.
- Bovine Bouquet: A lovely bouquet that makes sure your dream girl will never forget you.
- Cautiously Cattle: A light hint of dust, with a touch of sagebrush.
- Heavenly Holstein: A little touch of heaven on the hoof.
- Brisk Barnyard: For early mornings after a damp night.
- Dung Ho: For early evenings after a damp day.
- Barnyard Bouquet.
- Summer Sow.

The Misadventures of Granpa – Tell It Like It Is

I was doing a show in a mall for a huge group of school kids and at one point in the show I say, "What am I going to do with that dog?" At that moment, with the crowd perfectly silent, in this big echoie mall, this angry kid, who had to be about eight years old, stood up and yelled out, "Kill the ✱#☞↑⊗↓!X✱ S.O.B." Only he didn't say S.O.B., he said the whole thing straight up. I was taken aback as I am sure lots of parents were, but I didn't miss a beat. I said, "Oh, no. We're not going to do that. We're going to love

108

him and be patient with him and help him learn not to do that." And I went on with the show. Later a parent came up to me and lavished me with praise about my deeply insightful response to the child. I thought, I just said what my parents had taught me. No big deal.

GRANPA'S ICE CREAM FLAVORS

~ Chocolate Cow Chip Mint ~

~ Pigstacio ~

~ Bull Brickle ~

~ Swine Swirl ~

~ Sheep Dip Sherbet ~

~ Cowpatch Custard ~

~ Butterscotch Bovine ~

~ Rutabaga Raspberry ~

~ Cattle Nut Crunch ~

~ Farmyard Fudge ~

~ Chicken Cheesecake ~

~ Porkstacio ~

~ Bullberry Surprise ~

The Misadventures of Granpa – With Knees Shaking

One day while in prayer I sensed the Holy Spirit whisper to me, "Go to channel 40 in Indianapolis and be on their live, evening talk show." I was excited at this prophetic word from God and also very scared. A few days later I stood in the parking lot looking at the station and the big broadcast tower with my knees shaking. I figured when I introduced myself and said I wanted to talk about my puppets on their show they would just laugh and throw me back out the front door. But, I went in anyway and introduced myself. They took me in back where I shared some of my story with the producer and she said, "We need someone to interview tomorrow night. Can you bring some puppets?" That was it. Nothing to it. I went on, was interviewed by Lester Sumrall, and had a great time. At the end of the show the producer stepped up to me and said there was someone on the phone who wanted to talk to me. Turns out it was Vaughn Saum, who had just returned home from an engagement and happened to turn on the TV, and just happened to turn to channel 40 and see me on the talk show. It also turns out he was producing his TV show at that very station, the very next week, and needed to replace a puppeteer who had canceled at the last minute. That began a relationship that taught me much about TV. I went on to play characters, perform puppets, write scripts, and build sets and props for more than seventy five episodes of the Captain Hook Show. John Geddes also saw me on that show and eventually moved to Peoria to help me with the business and together we created the idea for PuppetmobilesTM, which created my success in the special events industry for the next forty years. Always listen to that still small voice, cause you never know what could happen, even if your knees are shaking!

GRANPA'S CROP DUSTER BIPLANE JOKES

Being an entramanure I decided to buy a bi-plane and go into business. To diversify I did crop dusting, sky writing and pizza delivery.

- ✝ I once dusted a guy's crops so low I had to pick the groundhogs off the wing tips.
- ✝ I once dusted a guy's crops so low I had to brush the dirt clods off my teeth.
- ✝ I once dusted a guy's crops so low the corn grew down.
- ✝ My airline slogan was: Fly Air Cratchet, where if you don't eat dirt it was a good flight.
- ✝ I tried sky writing but with the cross winds it didn't work out too well.
- ✝ He wanted Marry Me Suzie, but it said, Bury Me Floozie.
- ✝ She wanted Happy Birthday and it came out, Crappie death day.

✝ He asked for Will You Elope? and it came out You Need to Use Scope.

✝ The old couple Congratulations for their 50th anniversary. Instead it came out Coagulations.

✝ So I decided to give up crop dusting for pizza delivery. Have you ever seen an extra cheese pizza delivered at 300 miles an hour? People didn't leave to many big tips, what with the cost of pressure washing the front of their house and all.

✝ You can see how it didn't go so well, so I decided to expand and open an airline.

HOWEVER, PEOPLE KNEW RIGHT AWAY I WAS A SMALL AIRLINE WHEN . . .

✝ They asked for the bathroom and I open a port hole for them.

✝ They wanted soda and peanuts and I give them sniff and scratch samples.

✝ The terminal bathroom was a porta potty.

✝ I said please fasten your seatbelt and place your feet firmly on the peddles.

✝ They purchase an economy fare, I walk them behind the plane, hand them a rope and say hang on.

✝ I thought radar was a character on a TV show.

✝ I announce I need the landing lights now, so please turn your flashlight now and shine them out your window.

✝ To get service they had to self inflate a plastic stewardess.

✝ They saw me looking at a Rand McNally atlas.

✝ They by a one way ticket and it's for up only.

✝ The stewardess was still wearing her hip boots from her day job down at the sewage disposal plant.

Granpa Agriculture Quiz #26

True or false? A pig named Priscilla saved a boy from drowning. She is in the Pet Hall of Fame.

The Misadventures of Granpa – On Being Loved (Not well known. I don't care about that so much.)

I walked into a McDonald's just the other day in Cullman, Alabama and a family approached me and said, "Are you the guy that performs Granpa? Our little three year old girl absolutely loved your chicken show about work together. It's her favorite one so far." I said, "She's kind of young to have seen them all isn't she?" Mom said, "Oh, she hasn't seen them all yet, but I have. My brothers and I grew up seeing your shows at the Vinton County Fair in McCarthy, Ohio." Even now when I'm driving the Granpa rig down the interstate a car will pull up beside my window and honk, and a bunch of people inside will wave. I love it when those kinds of things happen. When I get down and discouraged I recall these instances and suck them for all the love I can. Thanks to all the kids; my own wonderful brothers and sister I helped my mom raise, my own kids who I had the joy of raising, and all those hundreds of thousands of kids all around the world who have given me the wonderful life I have. Hang on, the best is yet to come!

 ## INTERESTING GRANPA HISTORY AND FACTS #38

It is estimated that Granpa performers have spent more than twelve thousand hours sitting in PuppetmobilesTM talking to kids. And, another three thousand hours snoozing in them.

IT'S ALL PART OF BEING A SUCCESSFUL ENTERTAINER WITH THE WORLD'S MOST FAMOUS UNKNOWN CHARACTER, AND EVERYBODY'S FAVORITE OFF THE WALL, TOTALLY WIRED, ABSOLUTELY WACKO GRANDPA, GRANPA CRATCHET.

ONE LAST PARTING SHOT, FROM GRANPA AND SAM

FROM GRANPA: It's a terrible thing to have money and success and be depressed. Until further notice celebrate everything!

FROM SAM: If you don't like what you do, for goodness sake do something else. And while you're at it, make it about making people happy. Make the world laugh and you have it on a string.

Thousands of kids have visited Granpa at his front door.

IN CLOSING – A SPIRITUAL MESSAGE

I can't close this book off without sharing some of the faith that has made my journey possible. Often when business pressures seemed unbearable, when I was discouraged and just wanted to give up, my faith in the Lord Jesus played such a huge role in keeping me going.

I had a great upbringing in a Christian home, was taught to believe in Jesus, to trust the Bible as God's Word, to follow the leading of the Holy Spirit. What a journey it has been with the Lord at my side every step of the way. Every challenge, every setback, every discouragement, every victory has been an opportunity to experience God's presence, to learn how to pray and hear the voice of the Holy Spirit. Surely all these years I have learned to lean less on my ability and more on His grace.

All the thinking, creating and writing has taught me how to live John 7:37,38 and 39. I owe everything to Jesus. He died for me, saved me, gave me vision, insight, creativity and a drive that would kill a mule. Along the way He and I have gotten close and that's all that really matters in this whole journey. To know Him is to know anything is possible and to be close to Him results in believing the impossible for with Him there is no impossibility.

GOD HAS A SENSE OF HUMOR

While I have seen that God is awesomely Holy, I have also seen that He is very witty and has an incredible sense of humor. Truly, to know God is to come to the place where you can laugh at any and every problem. How is that? Because to know Him is to know there is a solution to every problem, even if you can't see it. So many religious people think God is this aloof, serious guy that can't be reached. Instead I see him as my Daddy; smiling, laughing, playing with children, and taking time to joke around a little and smiling with His disciples. I'm sure sometimes he had to smile at all their confusion when He simply did not meet any of their religious expectations.

I am so glad God has put me amongst the children as a life's work. Surely it has kept me young, lengthened my life and filled the journey with innocence, kindness, hugs, smiles and laughter. More than anyone you know I understand that we cannot enter into the things of the kingdom of God unless we become like these little children; inquisitive, open, pliable children of simple faith.

After living this journey I am convinced that God really is a very funny person, or at least He's not near as serious as religion makes Him out to be. I know I've matured along the way because now I laugh at my problems as much as I laugh at my jokes. Why? Partly because I know how big my God is compared to how small my problems are. And, I know everything the devil throws at me is a lie, a joke. I figure, hey, God laughs at my problems why shouldn't I? After all, a sense of humor is all about perspective, how you look at things. If God laughs at my disasters, maybe I should get a look from His point of view. It's a lot more fun than my point of view! Besides, when I got God's point of view I began to see that all my problems were actually my greatest opportunities.

GOD LAUGHS

If there is anywhere in your life where you are making your problems bigger than God then you are setting yourself up for a lot of discouragement. It makes it hard for Him to come alongside you and help you. When you fall into His arms with the faith of a little child and stop trying to earn His blessings and simply fall into His grace, He will then be open to gift you with what you need. I have seen it time and time again. Seeing God as bigger than your problems is the key to joy. Most certainly we much choose joy, but joy is not a choice it is a person, and his name is Jesus, and He has all your answers. Sometimes He might lead you to simply ignore the problems which stop your progress. Sometimes He may give you a new purpose to pursue which will help you get your eyes off your problems. Sometimes He might show you the opportunity that is hidden in your problem. In every case your problem will be your greatest opportunity to find true intimacy with God.

GOD'S VIEW

How did Jesus see the hungry five thousand? How did He see the dead child? How did He see the storm on the lake? How did He see a withered arm? How did He see the woman caught in adultery? When you see your problems as He sees them then you will begin to walk in the supernatural power of God. Without His eyes you will not see the supernatural and without the supernatural intervention of God there is no hope, no future and no joy. What the angel said to Mary, Jesus' mother is right, with God all things are possible! This is the outlook that turns disaster into joy. I learned all this from hundreds and hundreds of times when I would start a Granpa show depressed and defeated and end it laughing. All I did was ignore my problems and turn my emotions loose to have fun for twenty minutes and everything seemed to turn around. So I began to employ this same process in my life away from the Granpa stage. Where the mind goes the emotions follow. Anger or joy? It has everything to do with where you have focused your mind.

MAKE A CHOICE – CRUDDY OR FUNNY

I have decided to follow Him. You can too. This is where the joy is. Joy is a person. Connect with Him. This faith in God; it's trusting in His ability to solve every problem. This is where you learn to laugh at anything. It's where you choose if your life is going to be cruddy or funny. I'm sure sometimes it will be both. But, you can always choose to extract the funny from the cruddy. The crud is where many blessings are hidden.

When you choose funny your greatest problem becomes your greatest opportunity to know God. With this outlook you learn to laugh at disaster and plunge head first into the water of adversity, for there you know you will truly find His greatest presence and receive His greatest blessings.

God bless you as you begin to put your life in His hands, and trust Him, and begin to laugh again.

ISAIAH 55:12 – YOU SHALL GO OUT WITH JOY! AND BE LED FORTH WITH PEACE! AND ALL YOUR IMPOSSIBLE MOUNTAINS WILL SING WITH JOY ALONG WITH YOU AND YOU WILL WALK RIGHT OVER THEM IN TOTAL PEACE. (SLB TRANS)

AGRICULTURE QUIZ AND SHOW TRIVIA ANSWERS

AG QUIZ ANSWERS

All the answers to all the agriculture quizzes are true!

GRANMA'S SHOW TRIVIA ANSWERS

Show Trivia #1 - Spaz or Spit

Show Trivia #2 - Root

Show Trivia #3 – Fuzzball

Show Trivia #4 - Fee Fee

Show Trivia #5 - Pee Pee

Show Trivia #6 - In Granma's panty hose

Show Trivia #7 – Dispenses toilet paper

Show Trivia #8 - first

Show Trivia #9 - rule

Show Trivia #10 - garbage

Show Trivia #11 - work

Show Trivia #12 - instructions

Show Trivia #13 - the popcorn machine

Show Trivia #14 - chores

Show Trivia #15 - Rings a bell

Show Trivia #16 - The juice machine

Show Trivia #17 - Popcorn popper

Show Trivia #18 – He drinks his veggie juice

Show Trivia #19 - Sharpsville

Show Trivia #20 - The whole house

Show Trivia #21 - Henrietta

Show Trivia #22 – Mouse

Show Trivia #23 - Pack

Show Trivia #24 - Granma's birthday

Show Trivia #25 - Squirts the audience

Show Trivia #26 - Gives Granpa a big kiss

Show Trivia #27 - In Granpa's underwear

Sam, Anthony & Debbie

www.OLDCOOT.com

Granpa's creator, Sam Bowman is a bit of a humorous old coot himself! Named entrepreneur of the year, Sam holds a degree in psychology from Huntington University and has authored several inspirational books. Sam has also produced video games and music albums which support the wit and wisdom of the beloved Granpa Cratchet character. A proud granpa himself, Sam, along with his wife Debbie, are raising their grandson Anthony and hail from America's heartland, Indiana.

Granpas' award-winning show has been presented more than half a million times worldwide. Appearing with talented icons such as Willard Scott, Dick VanPatten, and Barbara Mandrel, Granpa has appeared on every major network and can be seen on the Captain Hook Show as well as the Kidz Television Network.

For information about bookings, to play games, watch video clips, or to purchase t-shirts, DVDs and CDs of Granpa Cratchet visit: www.oldcoot.com.

THE **ᗷOWMAN** INITIATIVE

Samuel and Debbie Bowman are the founders of The Bowman Initiative and are dedicated to elevating the culture of business and family.

Sam conducts mentoring groups and provides training and resources for those in business, helping them assess where they are and apply the principles of wisdom in practical ways.

Debbie brings her experience and insight to the realm of the home, focusing on helping women of all ages strengthen the fabric of their families and provide encouragement and hope for those who have lost their way.

Together they have brought Granpa Cratchet to life and help hundreds of thousands of children laugh and learn their way to a more positive future.

To learn more:

BOWMANINITIATIVE.COM

BRING GRANPA TO YOU!

Did you know you can book Granpa's award winning show for your special event? Granpa LOVES to make hilarious appearances at fairs, festivals, trade shows, corporate parties ... and more!

To invite Granpa Cratchet, all you need to do is send an email to sam@oldcoot.com with:

- YOUR NAME
- THE EVENT NAME AND DATES
- CITY, STATE, AND PHONE NUMBER

Sam will answer <u>all</u> your questions about cost and content. Sam's a pretty nice guy—and good thing too—Granpa needs lots of help!

www.OLDCOOT.com

www.ingramcontent.com/pod-product-compliance
Lightning Source LLC
Chambersburg PA
CBHW072006060426
42446CB00042B/2005